How to
Think

Sara Miller McCune founded SAGE Publishing in 1965 to support the dissemination of usable knowledge and educate a global community. SAGE publishes more than 1000 journals and over 800 new books each year, spanning a wide range of subject areas. Our growing selection of library products includes archives, data, case studies and video. SAGE remains majority owned by our founder and after her lifetime will become owned by a charitable trust that secures the company's continued independence.

Los Angeles | London | New Delhi | Singapore | Washington DC | Melbourne

How to Think

Your Essential Guide to Clear, Critical Thought

Tom Chatfield

Los Angeles | London | New Delhi
Singapore | Washington DC | Melbourne

Los Angeles | London | New Delhi
Singapore | Washington DC | Melbourne

SAGE Publications Ltd
1 Oliver's Yard
55 City Road
London EC1Y 1SP

SAGE Publications Inc.
2455 Teller Road
Thousand Oaks, California 91320

SAGE Publications India Pvt Ltd
B 1/I 1 Mohan Cooperative Industrial Area
Mathura Road
New Delhi 110 044

SAGE Publications Asia-Pacific Pte Ltd
3 Church Street
#10-04 Samsung Hub
Singapore 049483

© Tom Chatfield 2021

Editor: Jai Seaman
Assistant editor: Charlotte Bush
Production editor: Ian Antcliff
Copyeditor: Sharon Cawood
Proofreader: Emily Ayers
Marketing manager: Catherine Slinn
Cover design: Shaun Mercier
Typeset by: C&M Digitals (P) Ltd, Chennai, India
Printed in the UK by Bell & Bain Ltd, Glasgow

MIX
Paper from
responsible sources
FSC
www.fsc.org   FSC® C007785

Library of Congress Control Number:
2020950726

British Library Cataloguing in Publication data

A catalogue record for this book is available from the British Library

ISBN 978-1-5297-2742-5
ISBN 978-1-5297-2741-8 (pbk)

At SAGE we take sustainability seriously. Most of our products are printed in the UK using responsibly sourced papers and boards. When we print overseas we ensure sustainable papers are used as measured by the PREPS grading system. We undertake an annual audit to monitor our sustainability.

Contents

Thanks and acknowledgements

This is my third book for SAGE Publishing, and I remain immensely glad and grateful to have found a home for my writing there – and in particular for the encouragement and expertise of Jai Seaman, this book's editor; Charlotte Bush, its assistant editor; and the production team of Ian Antcliff and Shaun Mercier, who brought it to fruition on the page.

Plenty of others have supported me immeasurably at SAGE over the years, including Mila Steele, who commissioned my first book about critical thinking; Catherine Slinn, Amy Sparrow, Martha Sedgwick, Katie Metzler, Mark Kavanagh, Katherine Ryan, and others I know I'll be embarrassed to have overlooked. Throughout these strange times, Ziyad Marar and Timo Hannay have also offered me inspiration, support and friendship, and been among this book's first and most generous readers.

It's a remarkable privilege for any author to be closely read, and someone else who has given this gift is Rob Poynton, who not only offered insights that helped transform the text but also introduced me to other early readers to whom I'm tremendously grateful: Clarisa Doval, Janeena Sims, Gillian Colhoun and Alex Carabi.

Finally, my wife, Cat, and my children, Toby and Clio, have been and continue to be the largest and most precious part of my world. Thank you. For everything. Again.

Meet the author

Hi. I'm Tom. This is me, sitting at the desk in the shed in my garden where I wrote this book. Not many textbooks start with a selfie, but it feels appropriate here. This is a book about thinking, and thinking always comes from *someone, somewhere*: in my case, from a 39-year-old British man juggling work and childcare during the spring and summer of 2020.

Depending on who's asking, I tend to describe myself as an author and philosopher of technology. Since 2010, I've written half a dozen non-fiction books about topics ranging from video games to technology and language. Since 2017, I've also been writing textbooks and creating online courses for SAGE Publishing about critical thinking, a topic I've been passionately interested in since completing my doctorate at Oxford in 2005.

As you might guess from the above, I've enjoyed a happy and privileged life; and one of its greatest privileges is the opportunities I've had to reflect upon learning and thinking in the 21st century, and to try to create useful and accessible resources around these. In particular, I'm interested in the ways in which effective thinking entails not only reasoning, research and self-discipline – but also as much honesty, humility and empathy as we can muster.

The following pages, then, contain not only strategies and skills to help you become a more confident thinker and learner, but also techniques for dealing constructively with doubt and uncertainty – alongside explorations of my own uncertainties and limitations, of which there are plenty.

This isn't a book of answers. But it does, I hope, map a path towards something more practical and precious: questions that you can make your own.

How to use this book

Most importantly, I hope this book is enjoyable and readable: that you'll be able to start at the beginning and follow a clear progression through its ideas, arguments and suggestions.

I also hope that you'll regularly *pause* to question my claims and your interpretations of them. I've tried to build this into the book's structure in the form of regular reflective exercises. You'll also find key concepts spelled out in bullet points, and a conclusion to each chapter that includes recommendations for putting its ideas into practice.

All of these prompts are opportunities for you to consolidate your understanding, and to consider how your reading connects to the world beyond the page: to step back and see where a moment's thought may take you. Don't treat this kind of pausing as an indulgence. It is, I believe, one of the most fundamental habits of rich, successful learning and self-development. As the author Robert Poynton puts it in his 2019 book *Do/Pause*:

> In a pause you can question existing ways of acting, have new ideas or simply appreciate the life you are living. Without ever stopping to observe yourself, how can you explore what else you might do or who you might become?[1]

As you may have noticed, there is a numbered reference at the end of this quotation, linked to the notes and further readings at the end of the book. These notes and readings offer further details about the sources I've used, alongside comments and recommendations to help you explore each chapter's themes from a breadth of perspectives beyond my own.

The book's final chapter is designed to help you consolidate this reflective process: to look back on what I've covered, what you've found most useful, and what your plans are for further reading and research. You'll also find what I've called a 'toolkit for clearer thinking' after the final chapter. It lists ten key concepts that should help you put to work what you've learned, as well as providing a refresher for you to dip into on future occasions.

As all of the above suggests, I would strongly encourage you to respond *actively* as you read: to annotate, type or scribble notes; to capture the questions that resonate with you; and to debate and discuss your ideas with others. Don't take anything I say for granted.

Rather than devising simplified case studies, I've tried to draw real-world examples from unfolding global events, filtered through the limitations of my knowledge and experience. You'll have your own views about many topics. You'll know more about some of them, in retrospect, than I did at the time of writing. Celebrate, test and explore your knowledge. Be honest about how far certain outcomes were or weren't predictable. Be meticulous in anatomizing what I missed or got wrong.

Above all, keep asking what it means to embrace rigour in the face of complexity – and to put honest doubt at the heart of your learning.

How to Think

Introduction: Thinking about thinking

⇨ Metacognition and making sense of the world

⇨ Thinking together

⇨ Identifying and addressing your ignorance

Metacognition and making sense of the world

As I type these words, it's Thursday 26 March 2020. I am seated at my desk, at home, in the middle of the COVID-19 pandemic. It's a time of tremendous fear and uncertainty, but I'm one of the lucky ones: my family and I are well, so far, and able to self-isolate at home, on the edge of a small town about 30 miles outside London. Much of my and my wife's energy is going into looking after our two small children, planning food and deliveries, and trying to keep working as best we can from home. Given that my main occupation is writing, I'm doubly lucky, in that I can do this from almost anywhere.

I'm finding it hard to focus, though. The UK is in lockdown. Schools and nurseries are closed. The only people I've seen in person for the last fortnight are those immediate family members who live with me. My ordinary routines have been profoundly disrupted, and there's no end in sight. The website of the World Health Organization tells me that there have been 416,686 confirmed cases of the virus globally, and 18,589 confirmed deaths, as of yesterday evening, 25 March. I find it hard to imagine what it will be like to read back these words as this moment recedes and whatever is going to happen happens. But I know that it will be difficult to recapture the depths of the uncertainty that I and the rest of the world are currently facing.

To be human is to experience a constant tension between two different types of time: between our moment-by-moment experiences of the world, and the ways in which we remember and resolve these experiences into patterns. As the philosopher Søren Kierkegaard noted in his journal in 1843, 'It is perfectly true, as the philosophers say, that life must be understood backwards. But they forget the other proposition, that it must be lived forwards.'[2] The day-by-day business of living feels, at this particular moment, spectacularly distant from the ways in which I and others will come to comprehend these events.

Yet this is just an extreme version of something that is always true. Human understanding is always both provisional and belated. Many things that appear obvious in retrospect were anything but obvious at the time, because the clarity we experience when looking back in time is utterly unlike the cloud of uncertainty that surrounds day-to-day existence. The world is far more complex than any stories we can tell about it; far more mysterious, far harder to predict. Our ability to tidy things up into tales of cause and consequence is at once an astonishing and a dangerous talent.

Most of the time, as adult human beings, we do this kind of integrating and rationalizing so effortlessly that it seems as natural as breathing. Yet the ways in which we make sense of the world represent an overlapping set of competencies that, if we hope to improve their effectiveness and accuracy, demand lifelong practice and interrogation. In order to improve our thinking, in other words, we must take the time to reflect upon thinking itself: a process known as *metacognition*.

I've called this book 'How to think' – which is, it's true, both an immodest and a slightly odd title. Thinking is something you have always done and will keep on doing. What you may not have done so much of, however, is explore such themes as:

- *What* it means to think well.
- The *nature* of knowledge and understanding.
- The processes of *reasoning* through which people try to explain *why* things are the way they are…
- …and *what* is likely to happen in the future.
- The potential sources of *error, confusion* and *misunderstanding* that surround you.
- The particular modes of *critical, creative, investigative* and *collaborative* thinking that can help you build a more rigorous and less deceived understanding.

The following pages offer guidance, ideas and practices to help you interrogate and develop all these competencies – and to take surer control of your studies, learning and self-reflection.

Thinking together

Humans are not the only animals that think: many other species can do this. But we are unique in our ability to think collectively and culturally. Through language and the artefacts of the human-made world, we are able to capture and share observations about our inner lives and shared existences – and to turn these into structures with astonishing explanatory and analytical power.

Doing so is, however, fraught with uncertainties that we are all too adept at ignoring. As I type these words, the number of confirmed cases of COVID-19 in the world is increasing exponentially. What will happen next? What is the relationship between the number of confirmed cases and the actual number of infections? How accurate are the tests? How bad are things going to get? Reflection Box 0.1 contains some questions to consider.

REFLECTION BOX 0.1

⇨ Assuming you yourself lived through the pandemic, how did you feel at its start?

⇨ If you could send one piece of advice back in time to me as I type this, in March 2020, what would it be?

⇨ What do you think changes most – and least – in people's thinking during a time of crisis?

I can assure you that I'm not making any of this up. Everything you have read so far in this book was written on Thursday 26 March 2020. My children are playing outside in the sunshine of our garden as I type this sentence, marvellously unaware of the nature of the unfolding crisis. They are, respectively, four and six years old; and one of the challenges my wife and I face is how to explain what's going on in terms that they can understand.

This is a version of a challenge that every teacher and parent must constantly engage with: what does it mean to help children, and especially young children, to think effectively? How can you help them to understand complex events outside their immediate experience? How can you best prepare them for the world?

As soon as you start to explain pretty much anything to a young child, you notice that a great deal you take for granted when talking to an adult simply cannot be assumed. A bright six-year-old may know a lot of facts about dinosaurs, outer space or Pokémon, but probably has little concept of what it means to have a job, earn money, pay rent, or worry about losing that job and not being able to afford that rent. How could they? Even if some or all of these things have affected them, a child's understanding of what it means to 'have a job' will have little in common with an adult's.

To some degree, the same thing also applies to adults from different backgrounds or generations. Just imagine what would happen if you were sent back in time to the 1970s and tried to explain, for example, working as an Uber driver. How might you make the 2020s comprehensible to someone from a time before not only smartphones and GPS, but the world wide web? Or – to ask a more practical and urgent question – what does it mean for people from very different backgrounds genuinely to understand one another in the present day?

I've heard a number of commentators claim, recently, that the pandemic is a 'great equalizer' in the sense that a virus cannot know or care about the colour of someone's skin, where they're from, or how wealthy they are. While it may be well-intentioned, this claim is palpably false. As is the case for many diseases, factors like age, wealth and ethnicity are among the most important predictors of how unwell someone is likely to become if infected – not to mention whether they get infected in the first place, and how societal upheavals affect them. A single parent experiencing lockdown from a one-bedroom flat is living in a very different world to a family with a large house and garden. The experiences of those with access to excellent healthcare will differ profoundly from those without. Those with precarious work and few savings are vastly more vulnerable than those with secure, flexible jobs – and so on, across the whole spectrum of a society's inequalities.[3]

It takes little more than empathy and attentiveness to grasp at least the essence of these differences. Especially at times of stress and uncertainty, however, almost all of us tend to attach more weight to our own perspectives than they merit. Psychologists call this *availability bias*, and it describes something so obvious that its significance is easy to overlook. Unless we pay careful attention to the limitations of our knowledge and experience, our thinking tends to be dominated by whatever comes most easily and vividly to mind, no matter how unrepresentative it may be of everything else that's going on.[4] Spanning this divide – between our own and others' perspectives; between what we do and do not know – is a constant struggle.

This is why even very young children can be brilliant at maths or chess, but are unlikely to write great novels. It's easy to explain how chess pieces move, and for a child rapidly to build up chess-playing experience; but it's very difficult for a child to grasp the lived intricacies of the adult world. Similarly, it can be just as difficult for an adult to grasp that their experiences of something they take for granted – a home, a job, a family; their health, their race, their identity – don't directly correspond to others' experiences. And this is before you get into the deep divisions of sense and significance wrapped up within many words and ideas. Is calling someone a 'liberal' an insult, a compliment, or a neutral observation? It all depends on who's doing the talking – and where, and when and to whom.

This is partly why games, conversations and stories are such important forms of teaching. They create ways for learners to enter imaginatively as well as intellectually into others' experiences – and to grasp something of their intensity, variety and complexity. As the author Annette Simmons puts it in her 2000 book *The Story Factor*:

> Truth with a capital 'T' has many layers. Truths like justice
> or integrity are too complex to be expressed in a single law,
> statistic, or fact. Facts need the context of when, who, and where
> to become Truths. A story incorporates when and who – lasting
> minutes or generations and narrating an event or series of events
> with characters, actions and consequences… Story can hold the
> complexities of conflict and paradox.[5]

Facts, statistics and empirical research are of tremendous significance. But so, too, are the narratives and lived consequences that animate them; that mould them into competing claims about which things matter, and why, and what should be done. Reflection Box 0.2 contains some more questions to consider.

Identifying and addressing your ignorance

One of the most useful things we can do in the face of the complexities outlined above is to *seek to better understand the nature of our own ignorance.*

⇨ If you had to educate a six-year-old at home, what would your priorities be? Why?

⇨ How might you to try explain the idea of a pandemic to a six-year-old?

⇨ How might you help two people compare very different experiences of the same thing?

Although we may forget it – or may not like to admit it – we are all a little like children when it comes to our understanding of the world. There aren't many big questions that we know enough about to be able to answer entirely unaided. I'm busily writing a book called *How to Think*, but that doesn't mean I know the first thing about viral pandemics or, for that matter, about the practical business of educating my six-year-old son at home. What I do have, however, is a strategy for mitigating my ignorance. In the case of my son's schooling, it goes something like this:

- Be as clear as possible about the central question I'm trying to answer (*What's the best way of home-schooling my son during the pandemic?*).
- Spend some time exploring this question in order to discover what other questions I need to answer (*What is going to work best for me, my son and my family in terms of wellbeing and practicality? What should our priorities be? Why? What might help?*).
- Seek out some good content and advice from sources and people well placed to assist (*school, other parents, high quality websites, textbooks*).
- Keep on assessing and revisiting all of the above based on how things are going.

Most importantly, what I need to do is turn those things I don't even know I don't know (my 'unknown unknowns') into things I don't yet know, but that I'm aware I need to find out (my 'known unknowns').

Away from the delights of home-schooling, this approach also suggests why I visited the World Health Organization's website when I wanted to find a figure for confirmed coronavirus cases. I didn't know this without looking it up. If I had guessed it, I would (I think) have got the number wrong by more than 100,000. Two of the most important things that I did know, however, were:

- The specific nature of my own ignorance.
- A reliable method for redressing this ignorance.

It may sound too obvious to be worth saying, but all learning entails the admission and exploration of ignorance. If you're convinced you already know everything, then, by definition, you're incapable of learning. Six-year-olds sometimes suffer from this problem; as do some 60-year-olds.

Where does this leave us when it comes to the title of this book? Above all, I believe it leaves us in it together. We may be locked inside our own lives and experiences, but the world we share is one that can only be understood and explained through collective effort. And given that every aspect of an individual's life is defined, to some degree, by their interactions with the world – and with its people, systems and societies – this means we cannot know even ourselves without grasping this collective context.

To see the world more clearly is to realize, constantly, just how much you do not know; and to take careful steps to test what you *think* you know on the basis that, in the end, all human knowledge is provisional. This kind of *scepticism* may sound negative, even paralysing, but in fact it's the basis of the scientific method through which people have together constructed astonishing edifices of explanation and understanding – and have adjusted or dismantled such edifices in the light of new knowledge (just think how far humanity's conception of our place in the universe has shifted over the last millennium).

Contrary to some heroic accounts of scientific reason vanquishing unreason, I'll spend much of this book focusing on the limits of human reasonableness and understanding, together with the importance of introspection and of attributes often dismissed as irrational: our emotions, our creativity and empathy; our capacities for compassion and wonder.

Alongside this, I hope you'll take the time to keep interrogating your own learning needs, interests, habits and vulnerabilities – and the talents and aptitudes you wish to nurture. Some final questions for this chapter can be found in Reflection Box 0.3.

/// REFLECTION BOX 0.3

⇨ What are you hoping to get out of this book?

⇨ What do you consider your best and worst thinking habits?

⇨ What does the idea of thinking effectively mean to you, right now?

//

Summary and recommendations

- You need to make the time to actively reflect upon your own thinking if you want to improve. This thinking-about-thinking is sometimes called *metacognition*.
- Be as honest as possible about your limitations. Don't get into the habit of pretending greater confidence than you actually have.
- Learning entails taking a close interest in the gaps in your knowledge, experience and expertise – and what you need to find out (and who you should listen to) in order to redress these.
- Seeing the world more clearly means taking careful steps to test what you think you know – and being prepared to change your mind in the light of new knowledge.
- No matter how strongly you believe something, be prepared to submit it to honest scrutiny.

Attention and reflection: Building habits for better thinking

⇨ Doubts, habits and heuristics

⇨ Putting constructive doubt into practice

⇨ Time, attention and technology

Doubts, habits and heuristics

In 1910, the American philosopher and educationalist John Dewey published a book whose title was just one word different from that of the book you're reading right now: *How We Think*. It's both a foundational text for the discipline known as critical thinking and a sensitive exploration of thought in action – and at its heart is the business of doubt.

Specifically, Dewey was interested in the fact that serious thinking is an effortful, even a painful, business; and that it always entails some conflict between the desire for certainty (and thus for clarity when it comes to actions and beliefs) and the systematic suspension of judgement associated with intellectual inquiry. As he put it:

> Reflective thinking is always more or less troublesome because it involves overcoming the inertia that inclines one to accept suggestions at their face value; it involves willingness to endure a condition of mental unrest and disturbance. Reflective thinking, in short, means judgment suspended during further inquiry; and suspense is likely to be somewhat painful ... To maintain the state of doubt and to carry on systematic and protracted inquiry – these are the essentials of thinking.[6]

Dewey was writing over a hundred years ago, but his observations anticipate much recent research into the mind's minimization of the 'unrest and disturbance' associated with effortful deliberation – and the degree to which this conservation of mental effort is at once essential to our everyday functioning, and associated with a host of potential confusions.

Consider what happens when you get up in the morning. You may or may not have a rigid routine, but you'll almost certainly wash, dress, eat and drink in some order; and, on an ordinary day, you'll almost certainly do these things without pausing to give them deep consideration. This is as it should be. If such everyday tasks took up a tremendous amount of time and mental energy, it would be a challenge even for you to leave your home.

It's also unlikely that you spend most of your morning thinking profound thoughts – and this, too, is as it should be. In evolutionary terms, humanity's uniquely analytical intelligence is a costly asset: one that must, necessarily, be deployed safely and selectively. Committing to a process of systematic and protracted inquiry does not come easily to any of us. Our time, attention and willpower are scarce resources – which is why we rely on a combination of *instincts, emotions, heuristics* and *habits* to guide us from moment to moment.

Instincts and emotions are the raw biochemical basis of our existence: the rush of adrenalin we experience when a sudden noise suggests danger; the glow of oxytocin that comes from loving human contact; the dopamine release associated with learning and engagement; our hunger, thirst and tiredness; our pleasure-seeking and avoidance of pain.

Heuristics describe the mental 'rules of thumb' that we rely upon for most everyday judgements, and are interwoven with our instincts and emotions. We don't carry around a literal series of rules in our heads; rather, we rely upon factors such as familiarity, proximity and context as ways of efficiently arriving at safe, sensible decisions. When choosing what to eat in an unfamiliar setting, we're likely to go for something that looks familiar and appealing. When deciding who or what to trust, we're likely to go for someone or something we associate with safety and reliability. All of this makes excellent sense in survival terms, but has great potential for error and manipulation in the context of 21st-century civilization. Most forms of advertising and political campaigning, for example, seek to exploit such heuristics.

Finally, our habits describe anything we've done sufficiently regularly that, over time, it has come to require little conscious attention. Almost anything can become habitual, given enough practice. To paraphrase the ancient Greek philosopher Aristotle, *you are those things you most often do* – which is why regularly examining your habits is one of the most useful ways of improving thinking's foundations.[7]

Consider the questions in Reflection Box 1.1.

REFLECTION BOX 1.1

⇨ When and where do you do your best reflective thinking?

⇨ What times of day, places and habits help you to find focus?

⇨ What are your preferences when it comes to creative and collaborative thinking?

As all of the above suggests, thinking is as much a matter of the body as it is of the mind: something moulded by the spaces we are in, the routines we follow, the company we keep. This means it is only something we can hope to interrogate and improve if we address these shaping circumstances. Here are some questions worth asking yourself.

- Your time and attention are scarce, precious resources. What does spending them wisely mean to you? What does it mean for you to better control them?
- Examining your habits is one practical way of doing this. What do you habitually do that helps you be at your best, or find focus? What about a habit you hope to stop?
- We all need different types and textures of time if we want to think as effectively as possible. How can you best make use of different spaces, activities and contexts?
- Rest and recreation are important when it comes to replenishing your capacity for attending and engaging. What clears your head? What allows your mind to wander?

Perhaps most importantly, we need to remember that – so long as we are able to develop our capacity for interpreting and controlling them – our emotions, instincts and heuristics represent rich forms of apprehension, evaluation and guidance. They can leave us open to manipulation and confusion. But they are also fundamental to everything we are; and it is only by acknowledging and reflecting upon them that we can hope to follow a path of mindful self-development.

Putting constructive doubt into practice

Dewey's emphasis on the word 'doubt' may seem unduly negative as an aspiration. But doubting something *constructively* is very different from simply being dismissive, or claiming that there's no such thing as truth.

These positions – respectively known as *cynicism* and *extreme relativism* – do little more than evade the creation and testing of knowledge. By contrast, *constructive doubt* engages with the limitations of

Attention and Reflection

your knowledge or understanding, then seeks to do as much as possible in response. This requires several things that it's useful to express as habits of mind:

i **Attention:** Constructive doubt entails *pausing* to think twice. To doubt something constructively is to decide not to take it for granted.

ii **Curiosity:** Doubt implies a degree of *curiosity* and openness to new ideas. Pausing to engage in constructive scrutiny is unlikely to happen if you're indifferent, incurious, angry or fearful.

iii **Empathy:** To doubt is to believe that it's possible for either you, or somebody else, or both, to be mistaken; and this demands *empathy* with perspectives other than your own.

iv **Particularity:** Doubt should be *particular*, not general. It is always *about* something. Addressing doubt effectively means taking an interest in how it's possible to acquire reliable knowledge of a subject in the first place.

Consider the questions in Reflection Box 1.2.

/// REFLECTION BOX 1.2

⇨ Which of the habits listed above feels most most useful to you?

⇨ Why is this?

⇨ What might it mean for you to put it into practice?

///

Especially at a time of crisis, serious and sustained thinking is precious precisely because it resists short-cuts and evasions. Rather than retreating into wishful simplicities, it aspires towards a robust understanding of what is going on; and it acknowledges that such an understanding can only be built collectively and incrementally. In other words, it is the very act of acknowledging and embracing uncertainty that allows us to set about methodically reducing that uncertainty.

Hence my interest, in this book, in writing about current events. Textbooks are perilously prone to over-simplification. It's only too easy to come up with examples that make whatever you wish to prove seem self-evident. Even the careful application of doubt can be made to sound like a straightforward solution: a principle that any sensible person can surely manage to apply when necessary.

Yet, whenever I look at the wildly divergent ways in which the same people behave in different settings (myself included), I'm discomforted by the degree to which our behaviours are shaped by circumstances. We are creatures of habit and context: our consciousness and insights bounded by biology, society and opportunity.

What does clear, effective thinking look like within these constraints? Above all, I would argue, it begins with a close interrogation of our circumstances: our practices and shared assumptions; the tools we're using, and their defaults and biases; our physical environment, relationships and communities; the state of our bodies as well as our minds.

Such an interrogation isn't simply a case of intellect reining in instinct. As I emphasized above, our emotions, intuitions and heuristics are a highly evolved suite of adaptations – and it's in this history that we can find the best clues to both their strengths and their limitations. In general, emotions and heuristics are at their most reliable when:

- The context resembles those our species has been dealing with for hundreds of thousands of years, entailing limited amounts of information we can reliably assess unaided (*I know this person, and it feels like there's something they're not telling me*).
- We can draw upon personal expertise and insights that we've developed on the basis of meaningful practice (*I've been a firefighter for 15 years, and I have the strong feeling that there is something dangerous and unusual about this fire*).

Similar to many creative undertakings, these are the kinds of situation about which we have *valid intuitions*. They are amenable to a combination of innate and learned expertise – and, when facing them, it may be less than useful for us to overthink things. By contrast, we can flip these factors around to describe the kinds of situations in which emotions and heuristics often lead us into error:

Attention and Reflection

- The situation is novel in evolutionary terms, presenting us with overwhelming or unreliable information that we are ill-equipped to assess unaided (*lots of people are spreading stories on social media that make me feel paranoid about the government*).
- We lack the relevant skills and experience, or are encountering a situation that's too complex and uncertain for us to have developed reliable intuitions (*I'm no doctor, but I'm starting to feel kind of optimistic about the pandemic six months from now!*).

Although we may have strong feelings about situations like these, we would be well advised to pause – if only for a moment – and to seek reinforcements in the form of others' assessments, reliable external information, or some fresh framing of the problem.

Time, attention and technology

It has always been (and will always be) difficult to balance the daily demands of living with the conditions conducive to serious thought. But 21st-century technologies also present particular challenges.

Ours is an age suffused by information. And when it comes to engaging with this information, many of our habits are conditioned not so much by what's best for human understanding as by the design of the systems we're using. In particular, one of the great challenges information technology poses to effective thinking is its potential flattening of all our time into the same thing: into a constant semi-attending to the same apps and interfaces; into an accumulation of under-examined habits.

I'm conscious of this, right now, as I sit in my study typing. It's just after midday, and soon I'll pause for lunch and (lots of) coffee. I've been sitting at my desk, writing, for most of the morning. Or, to be more specific, I've been sitting at my desk trying to write while battling distraction and wrestling with ideas.

Contrary to a piece of advice I often give other people, I've also been checking social media fairly frequently, perhaps because I'm nervous about the state of the world. Emotions and instincts aren't easily set aside. As I write this, it's 1 May 2020 and the World Health

Organization has now recorded over 221,000 worldwide deaths out of 3.1 million confirmed cases of coronavirus. It's hard to ignore the daily drumbeat of statistics like this, partly because of their significance and fearful fascination – and partly because of the ceaseless flow of information online, and the design of the platforms through which this information is shared.

To put it bluntly, the business models dominating many information-sharing platforms focus on turning their users' attention into their operators' money. They do this by gathering as much data as possible, in the form of images, videos, comments, expressed preferences, interactions and other personal details – and then by selling advertising and services based on this data to paying customers.

How do you get billions of people to spend hour after hour sufficiently engaged to generate such data – and to serve as a captive audience? Above all, you tap into their strongest feelings and least examined judgements. Today, for example, when I look through the topics trending through the news and social media, I can see a passionate tribal conflict brewing around the origins of the virus: one that's generating billions of aggregated, saleable human moments.

This conflict entails (at least) three conflicting narratives. The most reliable sources I'm aware of suggest that the virus originated in China and arose via human contact with live animals near a market in Wuhan. This is the current verdict of the WHO, while the US Office of the Director of National Intelligence recently declared that it agrees with a 'wide scientific consensus' regarding COVID-19's natural origins. Remarkably enough, however, US President Donald Trump declared that he suspects the virus originated in the Wuhan Institute of Virology, and that the WHO 'should be ashamed of themselves because they're like the public relations agency for China'. Meanwhile, some of the most educated Chinese people I know are sharing stories claiming that the virus originated outside China, and that China is the victim of an international conspiracy.

I have no definitive way of knowing which of the above narratives is true. Nor do almost any of the people sharing them. What is clear, however, is that the conflict between these accounts is, first of all, about the rapidity and intensity of people's feelings, and only secondarily about evidence and facts.

I'm inclined to trust the first narrative both because of the lack of compelling evidence supporting the other claims, and because of the scientific consensus in its favour – such as a letter to the journal *Nature* in March from a Californian team of microbiologists, which stated that 'the genetic data irrefutably shows that [COVID-19] is not derived from any previously used virus backbone [i.e. it has not been created or modified in a lab]'.

What makes things more complicated, however, is the fact that the Wuhan Institute of Virology *does* specialize in studying corona-viruses that exist in bat populations – bats being the likely origin of the coronavirus causing the pandemic – and it has historically had some safety issues. Although reports of the virus being the product of genetic engineering are contradicted by strong evidence, it remains possible that a naturally occurring virus being researched in the lab was transmitted to humans by accident. It doesn't seem likely, but nor can this yet be ruled out. In a further muddying of the waters, China has been less than transparent about the first cases in the pandemic, and does exert considerable influence over the WHO. In other words, any verdict must at this stage be a provisional judgement based on the balance of probabilities.[8]

As far as many people are concerned, however, the 'fact' that they feel a particular way matters more than anything else, and the remaining details of the situation can be assessed on how well they match this feeling. This reliance upon a rapid emotional response under conditions of uncertainty is sometimes known as the *affect heuristic*[9] – and a combination of factors makes it particularly potent in the digital context:

- Doubt and critical engagement are time-consuming and demanding – but many online environments are suffused with (and explicitly incentivize) impactful content that elicits rapid reactions and crowds out more considered assessments.
- In the face of an overwhelming volume of information, it's easy to find 'evidence' supporting anything you wish to believe. Similarly, it's difficult to scrutinize any particular claim exhaustively.
- All of these challenges are amplified by societal uncertainty, urgency and threat – as are the opportunities for their deliberate exploitation and manipulation.

As this suggests, many online environments are a paradise for those who wish to mobilize people's passions, actions and reactions with a minimum of scrutiny or faithfulness to reality.

Yet this is only one half of a painful paradox. On the one hand, tidal waves of *misinformation* and *disinformation* threaten everything from the legitimacy of elections to effective engagement with urgent realities (*disinformation* is inaccurate information designed to deceive; *misinformation* is inaccurate information that may or may not have been intended to deceive). On the other hand, we now have knowledge and analyses at our fingertips that would have seemed beyond miraculous half a century ago. There has never been more high as well as low quality information in the world, nor more people working together to make sense of it. Both the opportunities and the stakes are dizzyingly high. What's going on?

Perhaps the most important factor at play is a version of the very thing Dewey articulated a century ago: we are all vulnerable to the *psychological asymmetry* between doubt and certainty. To see what this looks like in practice, imagine two statements on social media: the first expressing a high degree of doubt and caution, the second presenting a shocking statistic alongside a firm opinion. Now answer the questions in Reflection Box 1.3.

// REFLECTION BOX 1.3

⇨ Which statement is more likely to attract attention and be shared: the cautious or the shocking one?

⇨ Why is this?

⇨ What, if anything, might change this state of affairs?

//

Pretty clearly, the more striking and emotive a claim is, the more likely it is to be shared online, along the way provoking responses of equal intensity. Meanwhile, one of the least viral sentiments it's possible to express is: 'I don't really know what to think about this...'

What did you come up with in terms of challenging this state of affairs? Companies like Twitter and Facebook have, in response to

Attention and Reflection

recent mass manipulations of users, begun introducing elements of fact-checking into their platforms, seeking to slow the spread of dangerous untruths. Beyond the difficulty (and controversy) of ascertaining what is and isn't a dangerous untruth, however, it remains difficult for any cautious critique to compete with a headline-grabbing assertion.

During the early days of the pandemic, researchers tried to predict how bad things might get. It was vital that they expressed appropriate levels of caution when discussing future scenarios. Yet, as infectious disease researcher Adam Kucharski put it in late April, one effect of this was to create a 'vacuum for confidence' – that is, an opportunity for those people willing to express confident views to fill the psychological gap opened up by expressions of doubt elsewhere. The result? A profound media and political bias towards anything and everything that appeared to offer clarity.[10]

This is the problem of doubt's unpalatability writ large. At a moment of crisis, doubt can be deemed socially unacceptable, or even treacherous. It's the opposite of what experts, politicians and leaders are expected to offer. Should governments have closed national borders and ordered lockdowns sooner? Or will prolonged lockdowns ultimately cause more harm than good? To those recommending or ordering such actions, expressing doubt – let alone acknowledging past errors or the depths of present uncertainties – may seem at best useless, and at worst unthinkable.

Yet, as you might expect, it's my belief that the responses best able to help us are those that actively embrace caution, transparency and self-correction. The more wickedly complex the threat, the more urgent an alertness to these complexities – and to their potentially cascading consequences – becomes. A pandemic doesn't care what stories people tell about it. The Earth's climate isn't altered by ideologically charged assertions. In the long run, denying reality isn't a strategy that ends well for our species.

As I type these words, the world has rarely seemed more full of destructive certainties: of angry, fearful and self-righteous people determined to believe the worst of those who disagree with them; of many who ought to know better claiming a unique access to truth. Opposing such forces isn't simply a matter of caution. Sometimes, unambiguous injustices cry out to be redressed, losses to be comforted, and needs to be met. Sometimes, the sanest and most sensible response to uncertainty is decisive, precautionary action. But the route towards clarity is itself rarely clear – and is most likely to be betrayed by blindness to its obstacles.

Summary and recommendations

- Our time, attention and willpower are valuable, scarce resources, which is why we mostly rely on *instincts, emotions, heuristics* and *habits* to guide us.
- In general, emotions and heuristics are at their most useful when we have access to manageable amounts of reliable information, or possess meaningful skills acquired on the basis of experience.
- By contrast, you should pause and seek cognitive reinforcements if you're facing large amounts of unreliable information, a high level of complexity, or situations of which you have little or no meaningful experience.
- When our knowledge is uncertain or provisional, it's vital to communicate the nature of this uncertainty, and not to express a degree of confidence that the evidence doesn't warrant.
- Embracing scepticism and uncertainty doesn't oblige you either to dismiss everyone else's claims as self-interested *(cynicism)* or to act as if there's no such thing as truth *(extreme relativism)*.
- Aim to practice *constructive doubt* by taking a lively, curious interest in how knowledge can be acquired within a particular field – and how this knowledge can be tested and improved.
- Try to be aware of when you're relying on your emotions in the absence of evidence or experience. Explore what it means, for you, to cultivate habits that help you think twice about the things that matter most.

Attention and Reflection

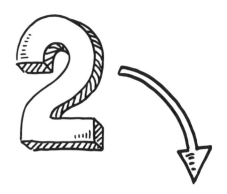

Working with words: Close reading and clear writing

⇨ The difference between clarity and precision

⇨ Achieving clarity in your writing

⇨ Rhetoric, fallacies and language online

The difference between clarity and precision

Imagine you've been tasked with explaining friction to a class of nine-year-olds. Which of the following examples does a better job?

- The tyres on a car wear out over time and eventually need replacing because of the existence of a force called friction between them and the road.
- The tyres on a car wear out over time and eventually need replacing because, every time you drive the car, a very small amount of rubber is scraped off the tyres by tiny bumps and lumps in the road's surface.

In my opinion, the second example is better than the first, even though it doesn't mention the word 'friction'. Why? Because, while the first example may look as though it defines a scientific concept, only the second offers any clarity about what is actually going on.

The first example says that 'a force called friction' exists between tyres and the road, thus introducing a technical term that will allow a class to demonstrate something that looks like understanding. How this thing called 'friction' works, however, isn't hinted at. Much like saying 'the car moved because of energy', the introduction of an apparently precise term conceals the fact that no explaining has taken place. Children are simply being taught to repeat words by rote. By contrast, the second example spells out the process through which a tyre is worn away.

I've adapted this example from the American scientist Richard Feynman, who not only won a Nobel Prize for his work in fundamental physics but was also (somewhat unexpectedly) involved in selecting textbooks for California's elementary schools. Feynman made a key distinction between clarity and *false precision*: that is, between explaining *how* something works, and providing a *precise-sounding term* in place of such an explanation.[11]

One of the best tests of a textbook, Feynman suggested, is whether a student can explain something in their own words after learning about it. I think about this test a lot, not least when writing books like this. It isn't easy to express things clearly. But the principle of finding your own words – of striving to spell out what is happening in careful, everyday language – can take both learners and teachers a long way.

Let's try it. Imagine that you now need to explain to our hypothetical nine-year-olds why something heavy falls to the ground when dropped. Consider the questions in Reflection Box 2.1.

What did you come up with? I would be inclined to start with concrete facts: 'When we drop something heavier than air, like an apple, it falls towards the Earth.' Then I would contextualize this with a larger, less obvious point: 'This makes it look like there's something special about the Earth, because everything falls towards it. But the only thing that's actually special is that the Earth is incredibly big compared to everything else around us.' Now I'm in a position to introduce a general principle: 'In fact, every object in the universe attracts every other object – but the strength of this attraction is directly related to the mass of these objects. Anything you drop is also attracting the Earth towards it, but by an incredibly tiny amount.'

It's only at this point that I might finally introduce the idea of gravity: 'We call this attraction gravity. The Earth's gravity is absolutely enormous compared to us, so it's usually all we notice. But the Earth itself is tiny in comparison to the Sun, which is why it and all the other planets orbit the Sun.'

What do you think? You may have taken a very different approach, which is fine. What matters is that offering an account of what actually happens – and why – is vastly more useful than teaching children to repeat 'heavy things fall to the ground because of gravity'.

False precision may be a bad thing – but *necessary precision* isn't. By necessary precision, I mean a degree of accuracy that's appropriate to your purposes and meaningful to your audience. If you're an engineer drawing up plans for a bridge, it's essential to be precise in your measurements. If you're a mathematician engaged in a debate with fellow mathematicians, you'll need to use highly technical terms.

It's still the case, however, that some engineers and mathematicians can offer far more lucid explanations of their thinking than others – and that those who just repeat received ideas may not understand their field as thoroughly as they think they do. In the introduction to his 1983 book *Intentionality*, the philosopher John Searle sets out a version of this principle: 'Where questions of style and exposition are concerned I try to follow a simple maxim: if you can't say it clearly you don't understand it yourself.'

Tellingly, Searle follows this with a qualification, noting that clarity can – unfortunately – sometimes be mistaken for making a point that's so obvious it doesn't require close attention: 'But anyone who attempts to write clearly runs the risk of being "understood" too quickly.'[12] No matter how clearly something is expressed, Searle suggests, it also needs to be read closely if it's to succeed as an act of communication. Otherwise, it may only be 'understood' in the most superficial sense. We can sum this up via two interrelated principles:

- *As writers and communicators*, clarity entails both explaining our ideas in a concrete, careful manner and attempting to prevent potential misunderstandings, confusions and hasty mis-readings.
- *As readers and thinkers*, clarity comes both from engaging with others' ideas attentively and, ultimately, from reconstructing their thinking in our own words.

As you may have noticed, this advice doesn't make much of a distinction between reading and writing, or indeed between communication and interpretation; something that captures an interdependency at the heart of language itself:

- Good writing is dependent upon good reading – and, in particular, upon becoming an attentive reader and re-reader of your own work.
- Engaging with others' work should be an active – even a creative – process, one which entails carefully converting their words into your understanding.

Achieving clarity in your writing

One thing I've learned about clarity is that, no matter how experienced you are, it is never something you fully achieve in a first draft. The process of clarification is iterative and, for me, it goes something like this:

i I plan, research and make notes, mapping the area I'm interested in until I've clarified what ground I need to cover.
ii I write, carefully, trying to anticipate my audience's interests and potential confusions.
iii I step back and read what I've written with a critical eye, trying to put myself in my audience's shoes. I may also ask other people to read my work to see what they think.
iv I do it all again, editing and re-reading until what I've got is good enough.

Personal priorities and preferences play a large part in all this, but there are also some overarching questions that help me clarify my thinking and style:

- Is the flow of my ideas clear and easy to follow, or do I need to shift their sequence – or spell out some implicit points?
- Are my sentences a manageable length and unambiguous, or are there places where they are too long, complex or unclear?
- Do my paragraphs contain, approximately, one main idea each?
- Have I assumed too much knowledge on the part of my audience: or do I need to provide more detail, information or explanation?
- Is what I'm saying sensible, coherent and well-reasoned? Or have I ended up making unevidenced claims, exaggerating, or leaping to unjustified conclusions?
- Do the words I've written actually mean what I thought they did when I wrote them – or might they imply something else?
- Is my style appropriate for the audience I'm writing for?
- When I read back my own writing out loud (which is one of the best ways I know of testing its style), does it strike the right tone?

I don't address all of these questions every time. But they do, hopefully, offer some sense of the principles underlying attentive re-writing – and show how trying to think yourself into the situation of your audience is vital. Try the exercise in Reflection Box 2.2 for yourself.

⇨ What, in particular, do you wish to improve or focus upon in your own writing?

⇨ Which items on my checklist feel most useful or relevant to you?

⇨ What additional points or prompts might you include in your own version of such a checklist?

//

For a concrete example of the process of clarification, see what you make of the following paragraph, in which I set out some advice around reading:

> Good writing is based in good reading, but this doesn't mean reading only 'good' books in the sense of worthy or self-improving ones. It means reading widely, passionately, eclectically, and with a range of skills that you're able to deploy as needed; it means exposing yourself to a diversity of others' words, and learning from them as much as you can about what it means to use words well. When I'm studying or researching, I tend to read with a pen in hand (metaphorically, at least: these days I often make notes on my laptop and read books in electronic form). I read in lots of different ways, not all of them close like this; but always there is the business of, when it matters, being able to focus in on the question of what exactly someone is saying, how their words are conveying it, and what my own understanding of this process is.

As you may have noticed, the language of this paragraph is quite loose. This is because you have just read a first draft, preserved exactly as the words came out. I haven't yet re-read and refined them in any way, meaning they are unlikely to be as clear as they could or should be. I'm now going to re-read and edit what I wrote. Here is each sentence of the original paragraph, followed by a newly edited version and an explanation of why I made these particular changes:

Good writing is based in good reading, but this doesn't mean reading only 'good' books in the sense of worthy or self-improving ones. → Good writing demands good reading – but this doesn't mean reading only 'good' books in the sense of worthy or self-improving ones.

I have replaced 'is based in' with 'demands' as it feels simpler and stronger to use a single verb rather than three words.

It means reading widely, passionately, eclectically, and with a range of skills that you're able to deploy as needed; it means exposing yourself to a diversity of others' words, and learning from them as much as you can about what it means to use words well. → It means reading widely, passionately and eclectically. It means exposing yourself to a diversity of others' words, and learning as much as you can from them.

I've cut the phrase 'and with a range of skills that you're able to deploy as needed' as it doesn't add much, as well as 'about what it means to use words well'. Ending with 'learning as much as you can from them' feels stronger and more direct, as does removing the semi-colon and creating two shorter, blunter sentences.

When I'm studying or researching, I tend to read with a pen in hand (metaphorically, at least: these days I often make notes on my laptop and read books in electronic form). → When I'm studying or researching, I try to annotate and respond to texts in my own words.

I've cut the references to reading with a pen in hand, and to making notes on my laptop and reading onscreen. These felt irrelevant to my key point, which is about annotations, not tech.

I read in lots of different ways, not all of them close like this; but always there is the business of, when it matters, being able to focus in on the question of what exactly someone is saying, how their words are conveying it, and what my own understanding of this process is. → I read in plenty of other ways, too: fast and for fun; revisiting old favourites; out loud to my children; slow and luxuriantly. What matters is my capacity for making meanings from words: for using them with confidence and pleasure, and continuing to learn new ways of doing so.

I have replaced the long and potentially confusing final sentence of my first effort with two sentences. The first evokes the different ways I read; a list I've expanded, as I think it adds depth and interest. The second more fully develops my conclusion. Here is the revised version of the paragraph in its entirety:

> Good writing demands good reading – but this doesn't mean reading only 'good' books in the sense of worthy or self-improving ones. It means reading widely, passionately and eclectically. It means exposing yourself to a diversity of others' words, and learning as much as you can from them. When I'm studying or researching, I try to annotate and respond to texts in my own words. I read in plenty of other ways, too: fast and for fun; revisiting old favourites; out loud to my children; slow and luxuriantly. What matters is my capacity for making meanings from words: for using them with confidence and pleasure, and continuing to learn new ways of doing so.

REFELECTION BOX 2.3

⇨ Do you think the changes I made improved this paragraph's clarity and coherence?

⇨ How do you feel about the style of this book, so far?

⇨ If you were writing a book, what style and tone would you aim for?

I've said that aiming for clarity is an iterative process, and this is true in more than one sense. Not only does trying to better express yourself demand re-reading and re-writing – but the very business of doing these things may also change what you're trying to say.

Sometimes, upon reflection, you may realize that you don't yet understand enough to do your subject justice; that there's something significant or interesting you need to find out more about; or that your initial conclusions were weak or incomplete. Indeed, much of the best writing and thinking is the result of realizations like this: those moments within you pushed your understanding a little further.

Similarly, achieving simplicity and brevity is often harder than writing at great length. This is because simplicity puts as large a burden of effort upon the writer as the reader. Length and difficulty, unless a topic or audience expressly demands them, are all too often the result of an inattentive or self-indulgent approach.

Rhetoric, fallacies and language online

When it comes to teasing out language's complexities, there is no final destination, and no such thing as a perfectly clear, impartial account. Like the processes of thinking and feeling they invoke, words are layered with meaning. Using them well means delving into these complexities – and training yourself, as best you can, to identify and mitigate against their distortions. Two areas of particular importance are:

- *Rhetoric*, which describes the *art of persuasion* – and, in particular, persuasion through emotional, tonal and stylistic appeals rather than reasoning.
- *Fallacies*, which are *faulty or mistaken assumptions* used to create the semblance of reasonable justification for a particular point of view.

Taking these one at a time, rhetoric may or may not be misleading, but it isn't inherently a bad thing. Indeed, all forms of writing and speech are to some degree rhetorical. Even adopting an apparently impersonal, reasonable tone is a kind of rhetoric.

Perhaps the best approach is thus, so far as possible, to evaluate the emotional and persuasive elements of language separately from its informational content; and to aim, in your own work, for a tone that informs and persuades primarily through reasoning rather than sound and fury. Here, for example, is a highly rhetorical formulation of a point I made at the start of this chapter:

I pity those poor fools who can't explain what something means in their own words: they haven't got a clue what they're talking about!

Can you pick out the rhetorical elements of these words? Here is the process in action:

i Set out more neutrally what is being claimed (that people who can't explain what something means in their own words don't really understand it).

ii Articulate the emotional thrust of the accompanying rhetoric, and how its effects are achieved (the rhetorical use of terms like 'ignorant' and the animated tone suggest that the author feels superior, consider those they're criticizing to be fools, and think that their audience ought to feel the same way, too).

The rhetoric in this example is an aggressive and quite possibly counter-productive assertion of superiority. Yet this doesn't mean that what is being claimed is inherently without merit – which is one reason it's important to separate out the content from the rhetoric. Even the angriest or most irritatingly expressed idea can be accurate in essence; just as the content of even the driest, most scientific-sounding summary can be wildly unreasonable.[13]

By contrast to rhetoric, a fallacy is by definition an inadequate justification. Here are just a few examples of fallacies which, in various forms, I discuss during the course of this book:

Appeals to emotion, in which people's strong feelings about a particular issue are misleadingly invoked as if they were decisive evidence. (*'I adore the president; he must be doing what's best for the country.'*)

Appeals to nature, authority, tradition, popularity, simplicity, etc, in which a claim that has some force in some circumstances is wrongly treated as a general rule. (*'A million people can't be wrong!' 'Things have always been this way!' 'The boss always knows best.'*)

Whataboutery, in which a point is dismissed on the inadequate grounds that there are other, more important issues to discuss. (*'It's meaningless to discuss legal niceties while there's a pandemic...'*)

Building straw men, where absurd caricatures of someone else's views are articulated just so that they can be dismissed. (*'In effect, she's saying that nobody should ever be punished for any crime, which is ridiculous...'*)

Working with Words

Conspiracy theories, which play off the idea that there's an ultimate hidden truth some sinister 'they' don't want you to know, and that all views that don't tie in with this are cover-ups. (*'Bill Gates is pulling all the strings, just you wait and see.'*)

Ad hominem fallacies where, rather than engaging with what someone has said, you instead imply that anything they say can be dismissed because of who they are. (*'She works in a hospital, so nothing she says about the health service can be trusted.'*)

Non sequiturs, where a conclusion is presented as reasonable but doesn't in fact follow from the other things you've said. (*'If I were rich, I'd be much happier. So I must deserve to be rich!'*)

False dilemmas, where two mutually exclusive options are wrongly presented as if they were the only possibilities. (*'Either we reintroduce the death penalty, or the nation descends into anarchy. It's a simple choice.'*)

Anecdotal evidence, in which a single example is presented as if it were decisive proof of a general principle. (*'They say eating junk food makes you overweight, but my friend Gary is really thin and eats lots of burgers; so it can't be bad for you.'*)

Above all, most fallacies offer seductive simplifications of complex situations. As such, they tend to be underpinned by an understandable desire to find categorical or reassuring resolutions to difficult questions – or to persuade others by proposing these.

REFLECTION BOX 2.4

⇨ Can you think of your own examples of some of these fallacies?

⇨ What, if anything, do the fallacies I've listed have in common?

⇨ Are there any fallacies or rhetorical manipulations you might add to my list?

Much of this may sound familiar from my discussion of the impacts of digital culture in the previous chapter, and with good reason. I've thus far emphasized traditional forms of reading and writing – but it's online, among the unanchored words of a digital age, that clarity and critical engagement face perhaps their defining contemporary challenges.

Many online exchanges can be thought of as a form of conversation without speech, bringing with them both the virtues and vices of the spoken and written realms (plus plenty that are entirely their own). Onscreen, words mix with unprecedented rapidity and freedom, mingling with other media, permitting a host of possibilities that include:

- Interactions and near-instantaneous responses.
- Enduring searchable and shareable records.
- Endless opportunities for cross-reference, representation and misrepresentation.
- The impossibility of unsaying something, or removing it from the record once shared.

Amid the internet's torrents of words, images and ideas, it can be hard to remember that clarity is even a possibility. The provenance of so much that's shared, said and shown is inherently opaque, or open to endless dispute. Yet, alongside the disinformation, manipulation and trolling, whole new modes and lexicons of engagement and analysis are emerging – with some devoted to skewering peculiarly digital fallacies and abuses.

To cite just one example, *sealioning* describes a form of harassment in which a victim is relentlessly asked to provide evidence and reasoning by someone who is hiding behind the excuse 'I'm just trying to have a debate.' With pleasing literal-mindedness, it takes its name from a 19 September 2014 strip featuring two 19th-century men and a sealion in David Malki's webcomic *Wondermark*. Having objected to something said by one of the men, the sealion starts to turn up in every part of its victims' lives, asking seemingly sincere and reasonable questions while refusing ever to leave them alone.

Sealioning is a strategy that allows its perpetrators to play the part of victims when confronted (*'but I'm just politely asking you to explain your position'*): a form of aggression masquerading as debate. In this, it typifies the ways in which reasonableness and sincerity are often performed, online, without any real interest in learning or exchanging ideas. There are countless opportunities for doing both of these things, of course. But finding and sustaining them can be emotionally and intellectually challenging, not least when anything you 'say' can potentially be decontextualized and used against you.

Perhaps the best advice I have to offer on this front (inadequate though it is) is that silence is often golden – and that taking the time to step back from the maelstrom is essential if you hope to take ownership of your thoughts. As the American psychologist Sherry Turkle puts it in her 2015 book *Reclaiming Conversation*:

> It is only when we are alone with our thoughts – not reacting to external stimuli – that we engage that part of the brain's basic infrastructure devoted to building up a sense of self... When we let our minds wander, we set our brains free.[14]

Today, most people's identities and ideas are profoundly influenced by online exchanges and performances; and there are endless riches and opportunities to be found in this realm. But, as Turkle notes, there remains a vital common ground between stepping back from such 'stimuli' – if only for a moment – and clarifying what we actually know, believe and wish to say.

Summary and recommendations

- It's important to distinguish *clarity* from *false precision*. Try to explain how something works clearly, in your own words, rather than offering definitions in the absence of explanations.
- Good writing is dependent upon good reading – and, in particular, upon becoming an attentive reader and re-reader of your own work.
- In general, achieving clarity means stripping away unnecessary obscurity, ambiguity and redundancy.
- Try to read back what you've written as closely as possible, and to anticipate any confusions on the part of your audience. Reading passages out loud can help, as can using printouts and annotations.

- Clear writing should flow logically from idea to idea. Aim for manageable sentence lengths, one main point per paragraph, and explicit clarifications of relevant information and assumptions.
- *Rhetoric* is the art of persuasion, and tends specifically to describe persuasion through emotional appeals. It's everywhere, and it isn't inherently bad or good, but it's important to be aware of its force.
- Engage with others' rhetoric by spelling out the rhetorical thrust of their approach as well as, separately, the ideas they're conveying.
- *Fallacies* are flawed assumptions invoked to make a particular claim or conclusion seem reasonable, but that don't in fact justify it.
- Fallacies tend to work by offering seductive simplifications, and by provoking rapid, intensely felt responses. Dispel their power by making their mechanics explicit.
- If in doubt, *pause*. Remember that your own and others' words can always be taken out of context. Step back from the maelstrom to take ownership of your thoughts.

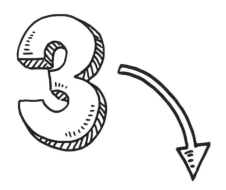

The importance of assumptions: Examining what has been left unsaid

⇨ Misunderstandings versus meaningful
disagreements

⇨ The assumptions that define us

⇨ Turning assumptions into investigations

Misunderstandings versus meaningful disagreements

Assumptions are those things we take for granted: whatever we don't explicitly spell out, but that our thinking relies upon. They're also extremely important. Indeed, it's the existence of shared assumptions that makes communication (and much else) possible.

As I write these words, I'm assuming they mean approximately the same thing to you as they do to me. It would be incredibly tiresome if I tried to explain every word in a sentence. It would also, in the end, be futile. I'd still have to explain my words via other words, my ideas via other ideas, and so on. Without some shared assumptions, there would be no common ground upon which to build either common understandings or meaningful disagreement.

While common understanding and meaningful disagreement may sound like opposites, they're actually two sides of the same coin. To see why, consider what happens when two people have very different assumptions. Imagine that I'm on the phone trying to help a relative with a computer problem. 'Click the button on the top right of your screen, the one with a little cross', I tell my relative. 'There's no button on the top right of my screen', they reply. 'Yes, there is!' I reply. 'No, there isn't!' they reply. Eventually, I realize that they think I'm talking about a physical button, like an on/off switch, while I am trying to describe an onscreen button that they need to click with their mouse.

In this example, my relative and I aren't so much having a disagreement as suffering from a fundamental *misunderstanding*. Our conversation can only become constructive if we manage to identify and spell out our incompatible assumptions. Until then, we're simply talking at cross purposes.

Innocuous impasses like this happen every day, as do less innocuous ones. Imagine that, once again, I'm on the phone trying to help a relative. But this time, instead of discussing computer problems, I am trying to convince them that they should allow themselves to be vaccinated against the coronavirus. 'Natural immunity is better than vaccines', they tell me. 'Vaccines are unnatural, they're toxic, they can overload the immune system. I prefer to take my chances without one.' 'No!' I reply, 'they work by prompting a perfectly natural immune response!' 'Rubbish!' I'm told, 'the government and big pharma make them in labs, they can't be trusted.' And so on.

One of the most important things going on, here, concerns several assumptions at work under cover of the words 'natural' and 'unnatural'. For a start, there's the assumption that 'natural' things are good and 'unnatural' things are bad. The kinds of sentiments that underlie such a position are clear enough: that 'science' isn't always right; that some traditional approaches may have more merit than novel ones; that novel treatments bring risks that may be incompletely understood; and so on. But it's equally clear that this in no way equates to a simple good/bad dichotomy.

If all human-made things are unnatural and thus bad, why is my relative wearing clothes, or glasses, or living in a house? Aren't there plenty of 'unnatural' medicines they are prepared to take, such as antibiotics and paracetamol, on the basis that these offer relief from perfectly natural (but undesirable) conditions? From pneumonia to broken bones to genetic disorders, plenty of natural things are bad so far as most people are concerned. In any case, isn't it perfectly 'natural' for human beings to do things such as build houses, wear clothes and research medicines? 'Natural' is one of those words that can feel straightforward until you try to explain it – at which point a host of complexities come into play.

Then there's the phrase 'natural immunity', which taps into the same set of strong feelings. Immunity can indeed arise naturally after someone has caught a disease, as a result of their immune system learning to combat it. But most vaccinations work by exposing people to deactivated elements of the micro-organism that causes a disease, thus allowing the immune system to 'recognize' it and gain resistance without a full-blown infection. Even innovative new techniques involving engineered genetic material are ways of teaching the immune system to resist infection using its own resources. In each case, the same 'natural' process underpins the immunity that's being conferred.

Statistically speaking, it is possible for people to react badly to vaccinations and become unwell – and there have been historical instances of inadequately tested vaccines causing real problems. Even if we factor in the worst examples of this, however, the number of people who experience such reactions is many orders of magnitude lower than the number of people who used to become seriously unwell or die as a result of the diseases vaccination programmes combat. And those studies cited by many people campaigning against vaccines, claiming (for example) that vaccination is associated with the development of autism in children, have been decisively debunked.

Moreover, all of this isn't just a matter of personal preference. Refusing to vaccinate yourself or your children doesn't just put you at risk. If you're in good health, your immune system may well fight off a disease like COVID-19 and confer some natural immunity upon you. But you're also likely to spread it to other people (some of whom may be far more vulnerable than you), especially if you don't have any symptoms.

Arguing that something must be good because it's natural, or bad because it's unnatural, is known (as you may recall from the list of fallacies in the previous chapter) as an *appeal to nature*. The flawed assumption at its heart is that the question of whether something is bad or good can be satisfactorily resolved simply by appealing to its natural/unnatural status. It's a common way of thinking when it comes to nutrition and health – and has some merit in some circumstances. There is, for instance, a case to be made that those foodstuffs our species has cultivated over millennia are more likely to be nourishing and safe than novel ones. This observation, however, becomes fallacious as soon as it's over-generalized and over-stated – not to mention exploited for publicity or propaganda purposes. Just think how many food and drink companies boast that their products are '100% natural' or 'free from artificial sweeteners and preservatives' as if this by itself guaranteed their goodness.

Ultimately, meaningfully addressing the question of how 'good' something is (or isn't) is about defining terms and gathering evidence with care. In the case of food and drink, this means addressing the circumstances of its manufacture, ingredients, effects, and so on. In the case of vaccines, this means digging into the best possible measures of their efficacy and safety – and the best lessons history can teach around precautions, side-effects and the politics of public health.

Importantly, simply to say 'I trust the science' is little more useful than saying 'it's natural and it must thus be good' – because scientific claims should, by their very nature, be open to evidence-based challenge.

It's vital, for instance, to be able to discuss vaccines in the light of rigorous research at the population level, because this is how the safety and impacts of mass vaccination can best be assessed and improved over time. It's also vital to look at the particular production and testing process behind a vaccine. An insufficiently rigorously tested vaccine may indeed pose some dangers. But carefully investigating – and mitigating against – such a prospect is very different from dismissing all vaccinations.

// REFLECTION BOX 3.1

⇨ What are your own views on vaccination?

⇨ Have they changed in the light of the above? Have I ignored anything significant?

⇨ How might you set about talking constructively to someone who disagrees with you?

//

As you've probably guessed, it's my personal belief that – if you're prepared to look into the evidence with an open mind – it's incredibly difficult to make the case that well-tested vaccination programmes are a bad thing. The smallpox virus, to pick perhaps history's most famous example, was declared eradicated in 1980; something achieved entirely through vaccination. Over the 19th and 20th centuries alone, smallpox is estimated to have killed around 500 million people. Since the last recorded naturally occurring case, in 1977, it has killed zero.[15]

Nevertheless, quite a few people distrust both this large-scale statistical way of thinking and the business of vaccination itself. Why? Perhaps because they've seen or heard emotionally impactful stories around 'what science isn't telling you' or 'the real truth about vaccines'; or because they view things like vaccination programmes as infringements of liberty; or because actively exposing themselves or their child to a vaccine feels like a needless risk compared to the 'natural' alternative of inaction. Perhaps – unfortunately – they may have painfully good personal reasons for distrusting officialdom's claims and promises.

Some people may simply feel too uncertain, afraid, angry or alienated to participate in an undertaking like mass vaccination. Some may have specific concerns around particular companies, institutions or research processes. But everything will ultimately be rooted in a series of assumptions around such things as health, nature, power, risk and liberty – and any and all attempts at discussion will founder if these underlying assumptions aren't addressed.

Similarly, for as long as my hypothetical relative insists that only 'natural immunity' is to be trusted, we can't begin to debate the actual risks and benefits of a particular vaccination. If, however, we make the assumptions underlying our disagreement explicit, we can in theory begin to discuss their truth or falsity, or at least how far we find them to be convincing upon reflection. Despite our differences, we can perhaps agree that 'is it natural?' is not a self-evidently reliable criterion for judging health interventions, or that the concerns wrapped up in a distrust of 'unnatural' treatments might be more usefully expressed in terms of shared anxieties around rushed attempts at developing COVID-19 vaccines, or the politics of their deployment.

We can do all of these things, and more; but only so long as we're willing to express, interrogate and (at least in principle) adapt our assumptions in the first place. In other words, what's required is for us to acknowledge that:

- No matter how self-evident they seem to us, the assumptions our ideas rest upon may need spelling out to others.
- Other people may have very different fundamental assumptions and, until these are also spelt out, we are unlikely to be able to debate constructively with them.

There's something worth adding to this list of admirably open-minded aspirations, however:

- In the absence of respectful, open engagement, we may enter a very different terrain within which mutual understanding is impossible.

The last of these points is, unfortunately, all too significant. Some people have little interest in seeing any resolution to a disagreement beyond their own victory. And some assumptions are so deeply held, or so inaccessible to scrutiny, that engaging with them requires either the permission of very particular contexts or considerable self-control – neither of which are in plentiful supply when it comes to societies' deepest divisions.[16]

The assumptions that define us

The more we see a belief not only as something we happen to think, but also as something that defines who we are – or that expresses a fundamental truth about right and wrong – the more we're likely to treat the very act of questioning it as a form of aggression. Assumptions aren't simply unexamined ideas. They're also the roots of identity and allegiance: the stuff of our personal and shared histories; our communities and our morality; the source of much of the greatest good and deepest harm we do to one another. That which we take as 'given' is, in some cases, nothing less than the bedrock of what we believe the world to be.

The psychologist Jonathan Haidt has spent much of his career developing and popularizing the theory of 'moral dimensions', most famously in his 2012 book *The Righteous Mind*, in an effort to describe how differing worldviews are rooted in a variety of fundamental, intensely felt moral assumptions. Haidt's view is explicitly indebted to the 18th century Scottish philosopher David Hume, who argued in his 1739 *Treatise of Human Nature* that 'Reason is, and ought only to be the slave of the passions'.[17]

For Haidt, as for Hume, people's views about right and wrong – about what matters, and why – constitute not so much a coherent, reasoned whole as a rationalization of various competing and sometimes contradictory fundamental assumptions. In particular, Haidt suggests six clusters of such assumptions rooted in attitudes towards care and harm, fairness and cheating, loyalty and betrayal, authority and subversion, sanctity and degradation, and liberty and oppression.

For the purposes of this book, what's most interesting is not so much this taxonomy as the degree to which differing priorities within it can help explain the difficulty of addressing some disagreements. How, for example, might you answer the questions in Reflection Box 3.2?

⇨ What do you understand by the idea of 'fairness' or of a 'fair' society?

⇨ Is it fair for a society to strive towards equality of outcomes for all, or equality of opportunities?

⇨ Is it fairer to redistribute resources according to need, or allocate them according to effort?

Most modern societies perform a balancing act between such principles as fairness-as-equality-of-outcomes and fairness-as-equality-of-opportunities. Where you think this balance should lie, however, will substantially depend on your background and experiences. There is no one definition of fairness so compelling that all people or societies subscribe to it – and there never will be. If asked, most people are likely to agree with the statement 'societies should have a fair justice system'. But this conceals the fact that what they think 'fairness' actually means will vary vastly.

Where does this leave the business of addressing our most important assumptions? Haidt emphasizes the significance of social norms and practices:

> We should not expect individuals to produce good, open-minded, truth-seeking reasoning, particularly when self-interest or reputational concerns are in play. But if you put individuals together in the right way, such that some individuals can use their reasoning powers to disconfirm the claims of others, and all individuals feel some common bond or shared fate that allows them to interact civilly, you can create a group that ends up producing good reasoning as an emergent property of the social system. This is why it's so important to have intellectual and ideological diversity within any group or institution whose goal is to find truth (such as an intelligence agency or a community of scientists) or to produce good public policy (such as a legislature or advisory board).[18]

'Good, open-minded, truth-seeking reasoning', in other words, is most likely to result from the constructive interplay of contrasting assumptions.

But this can only happen if there's both a common cause to rally around and a common commitment to respectful disagreement. It may be easier, emotionally and intellectually, only to speak to people who already agree with you. But the very fact that such *groupthink* allows you never to examine many shared assumptions means that you're certain, sooner or later, to miss out on valuable ideas and perspectives – and to fall into error thanks to your group's blindspots.

By contrast, explicitly articulating the breadth of fundamental assumptions held by different people is likely to yield robust insights, so long as rigorous organisational and evaluative structures are in place. As the American author and activist Marianne Williamson puts it in her 1997 book *The Healing of America:*

> It is our unity and our diversity that matter, and their relationship to each other reflects a philosophical and political truth outside of which we cannot thrive. Unity and diversity are not adversarial, but rather complementary … Both make us better. We are woven from many diverse threads; yet we are many and one at once.[19]

What might this look like in everyday life? Imagine you're working on a project with a number of people from different backgrounds. You're planning to invite a local business leader to attend an event, but your group cannot agree on how this should best be done. Some people feel that a formal letter would be most respectful and appropriate; some want to send an informal email; some want to make an approach via social media; others want to arrange an in-person meeting; others to suggest an online chat. Consider the questions in Reflection Box 3.3.

REFLECTION BOX 3.3

⇨ What underlying assumptions might it be useful to investigate in order to find out why the group is so divided?

⇨ How might you try to ensure a constructive exchange of views within the group?

⇨ What would a good outcome look like in terms of results – and members' feelings?

Perhaps the most important thing to remember is the usefulness of framing this disagreement within the context of a *common purpose*. In this case, the purpose is to find an approach that will be well-received by the business leader. Once everyone agrees that finding such an approach is what matters, the range of suggestions in play becomes an *advantage* – and the challenge becomes expressing and evaluating them constructively. Here's how this might work in practice:

- Having made it clear that everyone is on the same side, they all get to articulate their point of view, with no particular voice or perspective allowed to dominate.
- The group clarifies common points of agreement and disagreement, being careful to make this process as communal and impersonal as possible: the focus is on ideas, not people.
- Where people disagree, their different lines of reasoning are explained, so that the group can judge which is the most convincing.
- Where people agree, these ideas should still be debated and tested against the best available evidence, to ensure that as little as possible is taken for granted.
- The final course of action should be decided by majority consent, perhaps as the result of a vote.
- Ultimately, the most empowering assumption of all is that the group's success matters more than any personal victory.

Turning assumptions into investigations

Much as words like 'fairness' contain a multitude of interpretations, so the business of making assumptions itself has a significant double sense.

On the one hand, if someone tells me that I need to reconsider my assumptions, I may interpret this as an accusation that I've overlooked something important – and may react defensively as a result. On the other hand, things are likely to go very differently if instead they say to me: let's assume for a moment that you're right and I'm wrong, then see what follows from that.

Beginning a sentence with the words 'let's assume…' creates the possibility of a *mutual line of investigation*. This is one of the most important points about the relationship between assumptions and rigorous thinking, and is worth spelling out carefully:

- Any line of thought must begin with certain assumptions: those things that we both explicitly and implicitly accept as 'given'.
- A careful process of analysis can show us where our assumptions lead: what reasonably follows from them, if we assume that they are true or accurate.
- Given that we always have to make some assumptions, different lines of reasoning based on different sets of assumptions are likely to take us in very different directions.
- One of the most useful things we can do is thus to spell out both our own and each others' key assumptions, then to see what follows from each of these in turn. We can say 'first let's see what would follow if X is true; then let's do the same for Y…'.
- If we're sufficiently open-minded, this may help us to identify common assumptions, spell out faulty ones, and respectfully identify alternative perspectives.

As this suggests, correctly working out the implications of your own assumptions is far from the same thing as being definitively correct. If, for example, I claim that 'science is the only meaningful way of thinking about anything!', it reasonably follows from this that all spiritual, philosophical and artistic approaches are meaningless. Such a claim, however, says more about the limitations of my initial assumptions than it does about the power of my intellect. In other words:

- How we turn the world into questions, and the ways in which we frame our inquiries, matters at least as much as the results we obtain (and often more).

Consider the questions in Reflection Box 3.4, which invite you to try out several different framings of the same question.

⇨ Assuming that job satisfaction is the most important thing about any career, what would you advise someone turning 21 next year to pursue?

⇨ What about if you assume that lifetime earnings matter most? Or job security? Or contribution to society?

⇨ Where might a wise balance lie? What assumptions have defined your own choices?

As the exercise in Reflection Box 3.4 suggests, there isn't one right answer to a question like 'what career should I pursue?' – or, for that matter, 'what should I do with my life?' There are, however, more and less rigorous ways of examining the assumptions that underpin different answers, and of keeping life's most important questions open to experience and inquiry.

Let's return one last time to the assumption that asking whether something is natural or unnatural can answer the question 'is this a good healthcare intervention?' As we've seen, the problem is not that such an 'appeal to nature' has no merit. Rather, it's that its merits are being massively overstated – and its limitations ignored. This is what makes it a fallacious form of thinking. The world is being presented as a simple place where natural/unnatural distinctions are easy to make, and can unproblematically resolve complex questions.

This is the essence of almost all those worldviews that invoke one key criterion as a guarantee of truth or falsity. In each case, what's being assumed is that, because a claim has some force, it's possible to extrapolate a general rule from it. Just think of how often people rely on *stereotyping* to arrive at quick judgements. To rely on a stereotype is to rely on an over-generalized belief about a particular subject or category of person. In the absence of any detailed knowledge about Japan, I might assume that a Japanese person I'm about to meet will embody a vague few clichés I've picked up about Japanese society. In the absence of any detailed knowledge about publishing as a career, I might assume that it's like its depiction in a handful of movies and

TV shows. In the absence of any detailed knowledge about the virus behind the COVID-19 pandemic, I might assume that it's a lot like influenza – and follow this assumption far further than mounting evidence warrants.

In each case, I would be guilty of assuming that the world resembles a handful of simplified impressions far more than reality can bear. As the behavioural economist Daniel Kahneman puts it in his 2011 book *Thinking Fast, And Slow*: 'This is the essence of intuitive heuristics: when faced with a difficult question, we often answer an easier one instead, usually without noticing the substitution.'[20]

To constructively challenge a troublesome assumption, in other words, is to scrutinize something that has sunk beneath conscious notice; and to reinstate difficult, honest questions in the place of over-simplifications. This isn't easy, but nor is it impossible to do – or to embed in individual and institutional practices.

Similarly, to constructively engage with your own and others' assumptions is to flip the word 'assume' from accusation to investigation. It's to ask where your and others' worldviews derive from, and may lead; what a common ground might look like; and how far reality does or does not support what you think you know.

Summary and recommendations

- While *common understandings* and *meaningful disagreements* may sound like opposites, they're actually two sides of the same coin. When debating a point with someone else, always ask: do the words we're using even mean the same thing?
- Once we make the assumptions underlying a disagreement explicit, we can in theory begin to discuss their truth or falsity, or at least how far we find them convincing.
- To question someone's fundamental assumptions can feel like an attack. Try to be empathetic towards them, and honest about your own underlying beliefs. How far are they evidence-based? How far are they cultural and personal?
- Reasoning correctly isn't the same thing as being correct. Two perfectly sensible lines of reasoning based on different assumptions are likely to take two people in very different directions.

- Before focusing too closely on conclusions, make sure you've looked at where different lines of reasoning began – and at what may be incompatible in their foundations.
- To constructively challenge assumptions, try to reinstate difficult questions in the place of over-simplifications – and to seek not only an intellectual common ground with others, but also common values and purposes.

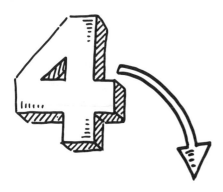

Giving good reasons: The importance of arguing your case

⇨ Arguments versus assertions

⇨ Premises, conclusions and standard form

⇨ Evaluating reasoning: deductive and inductive arguments

Arguments versus assertions

One of the most telling phrases of recent years was coined in a January 2017 press conference by Kellyanne Conway, counsellor to President Donald Trump. Questioned about claims made by Trump's press secretary, Sean Spicer, that the president had attracted the largest ever crowds for an inauguration – claims contradicted by photographic evidence and transit data – she responded: 'Sean Spicer, our press secretary, gave alternative facts…'.

The central contortion of the phrase 'alternative facts' was clear enough, with its suggestion that the truth was primarily a matter of allegiance. Conway was in effect saying: you have your facts, we have ours, and we have no more obligation to accept yours than anything else we don't like.

This is a curious way to talk about facts, if by facts you mean information there is good reason to accept as true. If, however, you've decided that a fact isn't something that's true regardless of who's asking, but rather something that a particular person is prepared to accept as true, Conway's response makes perfect sense. As she explained in a subsequent radio interview, 'People know, they have their own facts and figures, in terms of meaning which facts and figures are important to them.'

Above all, by talking about alternative facts, Conway was doing her job, in the sense that she was defending her administration's worldview from assault. Journalists in the audience wanted to discuss some dubious claims made by the president's press secretary. Conway didn't want to do this, or to acknowledge this as a legitimate topic. So she brushed off the question, then countered with a series of unrelated claims: 'Do you think it's a fact or not that millions of people have lost their plans or health insurance and their doctors under President Obama? … Do you think it's a fact that we spent billions of dollars on education in the last eight years only to have millions of kids still stuck in schools that fail them every single day? These are the facts that I want the press corps to cover.'[21]

Declaring someone's point of view irrelevant in the light of something else more important is known as *whataboutery*, another term you should recognize from my earliest list of fallacies. It's a staple of political point-scoring, and can be extremely effective.

If you bring up an idea that I don't want to address, whataboutery allows me to dismiss your point while at the same time claiming the moral high ground. 'How dare you suggest your topic is worth addressing', I effectively reply, 'in the context of this other thing that's much more urgent?' Whataboutery implies that I'm not rejecting your questions because I'm worried about looking foolish or admitting a mistake, but because I'm so concerned by other, more substantial issues.

As we saw in the previous chapter, this kind of manoeuvring is par for the course if your mission is to 'win' an argument at all costs. Anything that makes you look good and your opponent look bad is fair game. If, however, you're interested in investigating what's actually going on, it's essential to step outside the framework of partisan assaults and defeats – and to consider a different meaning of the word *argument*.

In philosophy, making an argument doesn't mean disagreeing with someone. Rather, it means setting out a line of reasoning in support of a conclusion. And while this may sound abstract, it actually embodies one of the most useful everyday ways people can interact.

Here's an example: if I tell you not to visit a certain restaurant because I got food poisoning there, I've provided you with both a recommendation and a reason suggesting why you should follow my recommendation. This is useful. By presenting you with a line of reasoning supporting a conclusion, I have allowed you to:

- *See why I hold a particular belief* (I got food poisoning at this restaurant: presumably, I think you should avoid it because I'm concerned you might get food poisoning too).
- *Assess how far you find my given reasoning convincing* (as long as you trust me, and if my experience was relatively recent, this sounds like a good reason to go elsewhere).
- *Compare my reasoning to your own, or to someone else's* (you've heard mixed things about this restaurant, and have never been there yourself; it's the only place serving your favourite cuisine in the area; but I seem pretty sure that its food made me unwell).
- *Make an informed decision about whether to accept my verdict, reject it, or investigate further* (it's probably a good idea to play things safe and find somewhere else to eat).

If, by contrast, I simply say 'That restaurant is no good!', I have presented you with an *assertion*. Unlike a claim supported by reasoning, an assertion offers no support for its own merit beyond the authority of the person making it. This is not so useful. By presenting you with an assertion, I'm forcing you either to accept or reject my claim based upon:

- *What you yourself know about the subject of my assertion* (you've heard mixed things about this restaurant; it's the only place serving your favourite cuisine in the area; I seem to think it's no good, but you've no idea why).
- *What you know about me* (given that I'm fussy and have very different tastes from you, you might assume that it's just not my kind of place; so you might as well give it a try).

By making an assertion, in other words, I'm denying you any insight into how I arrived at my position or why you might find it compelling. This may be a problem if you end up with food poisoning, especially if you would have behaved differently had I shared my reasoning. Consider the questions in Reflection Box 4.1.

REFLECTION BOX 4.1

⇨ When do you think it makes sense to accept an assertion?

⇨ When would it be most helpful to know the reasoning behind someone's position?

⇨ Do you think the reasons that people publicly offer to explain their beliefs are generally the real reasons they hold them?

Premises, conclusions and standard form

To speak in technical terms for a moment, every argument consists of one or more *premises* supporting a final *conclusion*. Premises are statements that, taken together, form a line of reasoning justifying this conclusion. We can use these terms to *reconstruct* my food poisoning example in what is known as *standard form* – a standard, simplified way of setting out the components of an argument, with its premises numbered in order followed by its conclusion (see Figure 4.1).

Premise 1	I got food poisoning at that restaurant
Conclusion	You shouldn't eat at that restaurant

Figure 4.1

Standard form aims to present an argument as clearly as possible in order to make it easy to analyse. In many ways, it's a formal version of the principle we explored in chapter two: that, if you want to ensure you understand something, it's important to restate it in your own words, in the process stripping away rhetoric and irrelevant detail.

It's also important, when reconstructing an argument, to spell out not only those premises someone has *explicitly* offered, but also any *implicit* premises that their argument relies upon but has taken for granted (an implicit premise could also be termed a *relevant assumption*). There's at least one implicit premise in the argument above (see Figure 4.2).

Premise 1	I got food poisoning at that restaurant
Premise 2 (implicit)	If you eat at that restaurant, you may also get food poisoning
Conclusion	You shouldn't eat at that restaurant

Figure 4.2

Does this implicit premise seem too obvious to be worth noting? Reconstructing arguments can look needlessly laborious. Yet, as we saw in the previous chapter, slowing down and teasing out relevant assumptions is vital if we want to think about something rigorously.

In the example above, the crux of my reasoning is not just that I got food poisoning: it's that, based on this experience, you might also get food poisoning if you eat at the same restaurant. Once we've made this clear, we can see that any factors mitigating against such a possibility may make my argument less convincing: if, for example, the restaurant has since undergone a rigorous inspection, or a change of management; or if my experience was a very long time ago.

The fact that someone has provided premises supporting a conclusion doesn't automatically make what they say correct. Indeed, one of the most valuable things about spelling out reasoning is that it can make weak or unconvincing claims easier to spot.

Imagine that, instead of warning you against a restaurant because I got food poisoning there, I said: 'Don't eat at that restaurant: I used to go there with my parents when I was ten years old, and I hated it!' We can reconstruct this reasoning in standard form, complete with as careful as possible an articulation of the implicit premise my reasoning relies upon (see Figure 4.3).

Premise 1	I hated that restaurant when I went there with my parents aged ten
Premise 2 (implicit)	The fact that I hated going to that restaurant several decades ago, when I was aged ten, is reason enough to suggest that you shouldn't go today
Conclusion	You shouldn't go to that restaurant

Figure 4.3

Once you spell this out, it's unlikely that even I would find my own reasoning convincing – at least if I'm willing to think things through rather than act offended. Moreover, if your analysis of my argument leads me to change my mind, this doesn't mean I somehow 'lose' while you 'win'. In theory, I actually stand to gain something. By abandoning an unreasonable position, I will (hopefully) be able to make better future judgements. I may even visit the restaurant and find out that I love what they've done with the place over the last 29 years.

This potential for clarifying and improving your thinking is one of the great gifts of expressing the reasons behind things. Even when you're thinking something through on your own, it can be extremely valuable to spell out your reasoning step by step. By doing this, you can identify where you may be confused, or relying on a faulty assumption; or where you don't yet know enough to justify a conclusion.

The greater the importance and complexity of a topic, the more valuable a reasoned assessment tends to be; and the more dangerous a perspective that's impervious to reason. Similarly, carefully reasoned

Giving Good Reasons

arguments come into their own when people disagree about some-thing significant that it isn't easy to resolve. Here, for example, is a line of argument making the case for something that's hugely contro-versial at the time of writing – the wearing of face masks in public during the pandemic:

> The virus is mainly spread via particles that come out of infected people's mouths, and wearing a mask reduces the spread of such particles, so governments should make wearing masks compulsory in crowded places.

Here, by contrast, is an argument against making face masks compulsory:

> Ordering people to wear masks might encourage them to be less rigorous with other, more important measures preventing the spread of the virus, like hand-washing; there's also little evidence that masks protect uninfected people from breathing in the virus; and we don't want mask supplies to run out for those who really need them, like healthcare workers. So they shouldn't be made compulsory.

Take a moment to read both arguments, then think about the ques-tions in Reflection Box 4.2.

REFLECTION BOX 4.2

⇨ What is the effect of seeing both arguments alongside one another?

⇨ Which argument do you find more convincing, taken on its own terms?

⇨ What more would you like to know about the topic to help you make up your mind?

It's clear that these arguments present two very different points of view. But it's also clear that the relationship between them need not be a zero-sum conflict, in which a 'winning' perspective is endorsed and a 'losing' one disregarded. As a result of encountering both, you might find that your own thinking on this debate is somewhat informed and clarified – and that you're left with some useful questions about what more you need to know.

Weighing up different, reasoned perspectives is vital for anyone interested in understanding the advantages and disadvantages of different approaches, and in integrating them into a more comprehensive analysis. It's also a demanding undertaking, both individually and collectively: one that insists we are capable of setting aside gut reactions and tribal allegiances and, instead, of asking questions whose answers may change what we believe the world to be:

• What is actually going on here?
• Am I right?
• Are you right?
• Does the truth lie between us, or elsewhere?
• How might we explore and test all of these things?

Context and tone matter a great deal, here. If I loudly proclaim: 'I'm not wearing a mask in public, I refuse to do it!' then I'm presenting you with a strongly felt assertion that, by the sound of it, I have little desire to debate or explain. If, however, I open a conversation by saying, 'here are some of the reasons that make me unwilling to wear a mask in public…' then I am treating you as a rational human being with whom I'm prepared to share and discuss my reasons – and by whom, perhaps, I'm prepared to be persuaded.[22]

Evaluating reasoning: deductive and inductive arguments

What does it mean for reasons to be compelling? Broadly speaking, there are two ways in which an argument can be forceful: one relating to logical structure, and one relating to patterns and likelihood. These are known as *deductive* and *inductive* forms, respectively.

The first of my two arguments about mask-wearing is an example of what's known as a *deductive* argument: one whose structure attempts to derive a logically definitive conclusion from its premises. We can set it out in standard form as shown in Figure 4.4.

Giving Good Reasons

Premise 1	The virus mainly spreads via particles from infected people's mouths
Premise 2	Wearing a mask reduces the spread of such particles
Premise 3 (implicit)	Particles being spread from infected people's mouths in crowded places represent a significant risk for spreading the virus
Premise 4 (implicit)	Measures likely significantly to reduce the spread of the virus should be made compulsory by governments
Conclusion	Governments should make wearing masks compulsory in crowded places

Figure 4.4

Notice that I've inserted two implicit premises in order to make the line of reasoning as clear as possible. How does this argument strike you, reading it in standard form, as opposed to when you read it for the first time?

We call this kind of argument a *deductive argument* because its conclusion can be deduced on a purely logical basis from its premises. If its premises are true – and if they are arranged in a *valid* line of reasoning, where each step follows logically from the previous one – then its conclusion must also be true. You can see this if you think of its structure in the abstract. If it is true that doing X significantly reduces the spread of the virus, and if it is true that anything which reduces the spread of the virus should be made compulsory, then it must also be true that doing X should be made compulsory. You don't need to know anything about X to know that the form of such an argument is logically compelling.

As the way I've set things out in the previous paragraph makes clear, the word 'if' provides an extremely important qualification when it comes to deductive arguments:

- *If* it is true that doing X significantly reduces viral spread and...
- *If* it is true that anything which significantly reduces viral spread should be compulsory, then...
- ...logic tells us that X should be compulsory.

But is it true that 'anything' which reduces the spread of the virus could, even in theory, be made compulsory? It would certainly reduce the spread of the virus if every single person in a country were ordered to stay at home indefinitely – but this has to be balanced against other needs.

In other words, the logic of an argument like this is attractive, but it's also potentially misleading – and we need to be careful not to confuse a logical relationship between premises with those premises' relationship to reality. In technical terms, we might say that this argument is *valid* but not *sound*, a sound deductive argument being one that is both valid and has true premises – and whose conclusion must, therefore, also be true.

By contrast, the second of my two arguments relies on *induction*: a form of reasoning based on patterns, likelihood and observation. We can see this if we set it out in standard form as in Figure 4.5.

Premise 1	Ordering people to wear masks might make them less rigorous at adopting other, more important measures preventing the virus's spread
Premise 2	There is little evidence that masks protect uninfected people
Premise 3	Making masks compulsory might mean that mask supplies run out for those who really need them, like healthcare workers
Conclusion	Mask-wearing probably shouldn't be made compulsory

Figure 4.5

The premises of this second argument support its conclusion in a different way from those of the first. In a deductive argument, we've seen that a conclusion should follow logically and inescapably from its premises: if the premises are true and the reasoning connecting them is valid, the conclusion must also be true. In an inductive argument, by contrast, the best that premises can do is very strongly support their conclusion in terms of likelihood. This is why I used the word 'probably' in the conclusion above. Mask-wearing probably shouldn't be made compulsory, the argument goes, because this might have some negative effects and probably won't do much good either.

An inductive argument is not aiming at certainty and can never be valid in the strictly logical sense, but it can be extremely convincing. We thus talk about an inductive argument being 'strong' or 'forceful' if

Giving Good Reasons

its premises make the case that its conclusion is probable – and 'weak' if they don't.

Does this mean that deductive arguments are better than inductive ones, or vice versa? No. In fact, the differences between them are something of an illusion. If we phrase things carefully, it's possible to reformulate any inductive argument in deductive form. All we have to do is spell out its key assumption that the balance of probabilities supports its conclusion. Once we've done this, the conclusion will then follow perfectly logically from its premises – because our additional premises spell out what needs to be true for the conclusion to follow. How we can do this in the case of my second example is shown in Figure 4.6.

Premise 1	Ordering people to wear masks might make them less rigorous at adopting other, more important measures preventing the virus's spread
Premise 2	There is little evidence that masks protect uninfected people
Premise 3	Making masks compulsory might mean that mask supplies run out for those who really need them, like healthcare workers
Premise 4 (implicit)	On balance, these potential negative consequences outweigh the potential positive consequences of making mask-wearing compulsory
Premise 5 (implicit)	Things should only be made compulsory if their potential positive effects on balance outweigh their potential negative effects
Conclusion	On balance, mask-wearing should not be made compulsory

Figure 4.6

Thanks to the addition of premises 4 and 5, this is now a valid deductive argument. Its conclusion follows logically from its premises:

- *If* it is true that the potential negative consequences of mask-wearing outweigh the potential positive consequences and…
- *If* it is true that only things that are on balance positive should be made compulsory, then…
- …it must also be true that mask-wearing shouldn't be made compulsory.

This doesn't make this claim any truer than before, of course. It simply leaves us in the same position as we were in relation to the first, deductive argument: obliged to assess the truth of statements qualified by the word 'if'.

Does this mean we haven't made any progress? No. We haven't magically gained certainty – but we may have gained clarity. Spelling out inductive arguments in deductive form can be a useful way of evaluating the assumptions of likelihood and causal relations that they rely upon.

Having meticulously reconstructed both arguments, we now have an excellent basis for comparing their strengths and weaknesses – and for asking what else we might need to know before accepting or rejecting part or all of them. Consider the questions in Reflection Box 4.3.

REFLECTION BOX 4.3

⇨ Have you changed your mind about the relative strengths and weaknesses of these arguments?

⇨ If so, why?

⇨ What additional information might you now want to know about this subject?

In my opinion – which may not be yours – the second argument is weaker than the first, because each of its premises raises a concern that can be mitigated against.

Ordering people to wear masks might make them less rigorous at adopting other measures; but not, hopefully, if public messaging is done clearly and effectively. Any evidence that masks may not protect uninfected people from exposure to the virus should be borne in mind – but their great benefit, as the first argument makes clear, is that they can block some of the particles released by infected people, and that blocking such particles is likely to make crowded spaces safer. Reserving mask supplies for healthcare and other essential workers is important – but this too can be mitigated against by encouraging people to make or wear simpler coverings (which still block some

Giving Good Reasons

particles), while reserving high-grade medical masks for those who need them most.

You may disagree with this analysis – and a huge question begged by both of the arguments above is what the best research into the effects of mask-wearing shows in real-world conditions – but the point remains that a close examination of two different arguments can help us to test and adapt our own views (and that this process is considerably more informative than an angry exchange of assertions). Try it for yourself. What might the following argument look like when reconstructed in standard form – and how convincing do you find it?

> I'm young and healthy, I live on my own, there's no problem with me choosing not to wear a mask in public. It's up to me whether I risk my health, and nobody else.

I've provided some implicit premises, leaving you to fill in the explicit ones, in Figure 4.7.

Premise 1	_____
Premise 2 (implicit)	As a young and healthy person, I am unlikely to become seriously ill even if I am infected with COVID-19
Premise 3	_____
Premise 4 (implicit)	Because I live alone, I am not putting anyone else at risk by not wearing a mask in public
Premise 5	_____
Premise 6 (implicit)	The health risks posed by COVID-19 are solely my business, and nobody else has a right to insist upon my wearing a mask
Conclusion	_____

Figure 4.7

My completed version can be found in Figure 4.8.

Premise 1	I am young and healthy
Premise 2 (implicit)	As a young and healthy person, I am unlikely to become seriously ill even if I am infected with COVID-19
Premise 3	I live alone
Premise 4 (implicit)	Because I live alone, I am not putting anyone else at risk by not wearing a mask in public

(Continued)

Figure 4.8 (Continued)

Premise 5	It is up to me, and only me, whether I risk my health
Premise 6 (implicit)	The health risks posed by COVID-19 are solely my business, and nobody else has a right to insist upon, e.g., my wearing a mask
Conclusion	There is no problem with me choosing not to wear a mask in public

Figure 4.8

As the number of implicit premises in my reconstruction suggests, a great deal of work is being done by unspoken assumptions – as is often the case when it comes to everyday language. Indeed, one of the main tasks (and promises) of formal reasoning is that it can make the connections between everyday ideas explicit and assessable, at least in principle; and that, where there are contradictions or omissions, it can invite us to reflect upon these, then work towards a more rigorous and comprehensive account.[23]

As to the merits of this argument, I'd suggest that even the most generous interpretation of its assumptions doesn't yield a convincing line of inductive reasoning, because it ignores the potential of young, asymptomatic people to spread the disease when they're out in public. It also – as the next chapter explores – further highlights the need for rigorous *research* when it comes to working out what's going on. If you're only interested in thinking yourself correct, it's possible to make an argument in favour of pretty much anything.

What do you think? What do effective, justifiable and proportionate public health measures look like – and how can those enacting them gain public support? Self-evidently, there are no easy answers to such questions. And this is precisely why what's most urgently needed is an ongoing, respectful and evidence-based debate.[24]

Summary and recommendations

- If your mission is to win an argument at all costs, anything that makes you look good or your opponent look bad is fair game. If you're interested in something beyond victory at all costs, it's essential to step outside this framing.

- In philosophy, an *argument* isn't simply a disagreement. Instead, it entails setting out one or more *premises* to form a line of reasoning justifying a *conclusion*.
- By contrast, an *assertion* simply states that something is the case, without justification or explanation.
- Spelling out the reasoning behind something allows you to see *why* someone believes it, assess *how convincing* you find this reasoning, *compare* it to other lines of reasoning – and thus to make an *informed decision* about whether to accept it.
- *Reconstructing* an argument in *standard form* entails setting out its premises in order, including any *implicit premises* it relies upon, followed by its final conclusion.
- A *valid deductive argument* is one whose conclusion follows logically from its premises. If a valid deductive argument's premises are true, its conclusion must be true as well, and it is said to be *sound*.
- But don't be seduced by the apparent certainty of perfectly logical statements that turn out to be based on over-simplified or untrue premises.
- An *inductive* argument is based on observations of real-world evidence and patterns, and is *strong* if its premises show its conclusion is very likely to be true.
- An inductive argument cannot be valid or prove its conclusion definitively to be true, but it can offer very strong reasons to accept something.
- Any inductive argument can be expressed as a deductive argument if its assumptions about the balance of probabilities are made explicit. This doesn't create certainty, but it can usefully clarify what is being claimed, and why.

Seeking good explanations: Investigating the reasons behind things

⇨ Straw men and the principle of charity

⇨ Coming up with explanations

⇨ Testing rival explanations

Straw men and the principle of charity

There's something paradoxical about the power of reasoning. The more you disagree with someone – or the more different their worldview is from yours – the more valuable it often is to be as thorough as possible when considering their perspective. To understand why, consider the alternative. Imagine that someone presents me with this observation:

> Based on the feedback I've seen, if you don't update your course to better reflect students' lives and experiences, you may end up with very few wanting to take it.

How should I react? Here's one possible response:

> So you're claiming that the only way to keep students interested in my course is to make it all about them? I'm not prepared to pander to their self-absorption. My course doesn't need updating: the whole point is to teach students things they don't know.

Is this fair? Now consider this response instead:

> So you're suggesting that the current course materials aren't easy for students to relate to – and that there are ways I could draw upon their lives and experiences to make it more accessible and engaging? If what you say about them losing interest in taking the course is correct, it does sound like I should look into this.

Which response do you think is more reasonable? It can be difficult to handle criticism well. But, as the contrast between the two responses hopefully suggests, there are also some problems with the first way of reacting.

Rather than treating the speaker's position as a line of reasoning to be engaged with, this first response instead treats it as an assault that needs to be defended against – much as we saw in the example of *whataboutery* in the previous chapter. In this case, a different technique from our list of fallacies is being deployed: *building a straw man*. This entails constructing an over-simplified version of someone else's point of view just so that you can dismiss it, as if you were building a straw figure to be symbolically destroyed. It's an approach that shouldn't survive honest scrutiny – but one that, like many strategies for evading reasoned debate, can be effective at preventing this scrutiny from happening.

Once we look closely at the initial observation and the straw man response, it's clear that updating a course to better reflect students' lives and experiences doesn't necessarily mean 'making it all about them' – and that misrepresenting it like this makes it easy to ignore the point being made. Similarly, the accusation that students must be suffering from 'self-absorption' is gratuitous: it portrays criticism as self-indulgent and thus not worth taking seriously.

By contrast, the second response takes on board what is being said, based on the assumption that there may well be reasonable issues underpinning students' feedback. Is this the same as admitting that the criticism must be valid? No. It may turn out that, upon further investigation, plenty of students do love the course and consider it highly relevant; or that it's some entirely different factor that's putting people off.

The point is that, precisely because we can't know things like this in advance, they are worthy of investigation. Moreover – if I'm actually interested in designing a course that is as effective and well-subscribed as possible – discovering potential problems is far more valuable than receiving feedback that says 'it's all fine'. In much the same way as learning requires us to admit ignorance, improvement requires us to take an interest in what isn't currently working, or could work better.[25]

One technique for applying this principle in practice is to turn other people's ideas into what's sometimes called a *steel man*: that is, to construct the strongest possible version of their argument. This sounds counter-intuitive, but has several advantages:

- If you hope to persuade or find common cause with those who disagree with you (rather than dismiss them), you need to learn as much about their position as possible.
- By ensuring you encounter the strongest possible version of someone else's perspective, a steel man ensures you maximize your ability to learn from it.
- Engaging with the strongest form of a perspective you disagree with (or haven't previously considered) means that your own strongly held ideas must pass a meaningful test.

To idealize, one of the most productive ways you can engage with others is to re-state their ideas in a way that they agree is fair – and only then, once you've done this, to explain where you do and don't agree with them, and why. This approach is sometimes called *the principle of charity*. The word 'charity' may sound strange in such a context, but the principle itself is one of our oldest and most practical guides to reasoned debate. It exists in various formulations, all rooted in the same idea:

> So far as possible, you should try to extract the maximum possible truthful and reasonable content from what others say, especially if they disagree with you.

Here is an exercise that goes back to the ancient Greeks, and remains well worth practising today. First of all, think of a position that you strongly disagree with. Done? Now consider the questions in Reflection Box 5.1.

REFLECTION BOX 5.1

⇨ What are the strongest possible justifications for such a position?

⇨ Can you counter all of these justifications convincingly?

⇨ Does anything that you've come up with challenge or change what you think is right?

Note that the principle of charity extends not only to *what* someone is saying, but also to your assumptions around *why* they are saying it. We can put this explicitly:

> Unless you have decisive evidence to the contrary, you should start off by assuming that someone else's position is reasonable and sincerely held, rather than that they are malicious, ignorant or mistaken.

Why? Once again, the answer isn't because this is a nice thing to do (although it may be), but because it's only by beginning with charitable assumptions that you can get to grips with the underpinnings of someone else's perspective – and ensure that any condemnation you may eventually make of their motives is based on a careful, fair-minded assessment.

Such condemnations will generally be *more* rather than *less* forceful than those based on prejudice or burning straw men. And they should also ensure that you've had the best possible opportunity to identify any errors and limitations in your own thinking. All of which handily brings us into the realm of explanations, evidence, and meaningful tests.

Coming up with explanations

In some ways, explanations are the opposite of arguments. When making an argument, we move from one or more initial premises that we believe to be true towards a final conclusion that, so long as our argument is a convincing one, we believe it's reasonable to accept as true. But we can also flip this sequence around, beginning with something we believe to be true and then asking 'how did things come to be this way?' In other words:

- The central question of an argument is: '*What follows if* X is the case?'
- An explanation instead asks: 'I know that X is the case – *but why is this so?*'

This immediately presents us with a challenge. The conclusion of a well-reasoned argument should self-evidently follow from its premises. But it's much less clear what it means satisfactorily to address a question beginning with 'why?' Consider what can happen when you're explaining something to a child who is fond of this word:

Why did the apple fall from the tree? Because the stem supporting it snapped.

Why did it fall when the stem snapped? Because it was attracted towards the Earth by the force of gravity.

Why was it attracted towards the Earth by the force of gravity? Because what we call gravity is one of the fundamental forces that dictate how matter in our universe behaves; and this behaviour includes an attraction caused by mass.

Why is gravity a fundamental force? We don't know – but we do know that, if things behaved differently, we probably wouldn't be around to observe them.

Why? Because I say so.

There is no limit to the number of times 'why' can be asked – or ways it can be answered. Fortunately, however, the general principles of good explanations are simple enough. In addition to being relevant or useful to the questioner, a good explanation tends to do two things:

- . It accounts for all the relevant information we know.
- It does this while being as simple as possible.

By contrast, a bad explanation generally does the opposite:

- It ignores whatever is inconvenient.
- It is unnecessarily complex.

These principles can help us understand what, for example, is so troubling about conspiracy theories. Here's one alarmingly widespread current example, connecting 5G mobile phone masts (the 5G stands for 'fifth generation') and the coronavirus pandemic:

> Why is there a pandemic? Next-generation 5G phone masts began being rolled out in large numbers globally in 2019. At the end of the year, the coronavirus outbreak began in China. Shadowy global elites are using 5G radiation to weaken people's immune systems and help spread the virus.

What do you think of this theory? First, it's useful to compare it to a non-conspiratorial account of events:

> Why is there a pandemic? The novel coronavirus outbreak began at the end of 2019 in China when a virus crossed over from animals to humans. Despite efforts at containment, its spread – especially via those who were contagious but hadn't yet developed symptoms – followed regional and then global travel routes, fuelled by so-called 'superspreading events'.

Which account do you think best fits the criteria for a good explanation? Like most conspiracy theories, the 5G one is flawed in several key respects. It ignores or distorts inconvenient evidence, including almost everything we know about how viruses, immune systems and electromagnetic radiation work; it invokes the existence of a vast and intricate (yet somehow still secret) global conspiracy that is many orders of magnitude more complex than other explanations; and it has almost no power or precision when it comes to making predictions.

Part of the appeal of a conspiracy theory, of course, is precisely that it can be extended to encompass pretty much anything; that it presents the world in stark terms of good and lurking evil; and that its myth-making gives people permission to ignore reality's complexities and uncertainties. In this context, it's only too easy to see why conspiracy theories proliferate at times of trouble. The idea that a hidden, definitive truth lies within a handful of lurid websites can be far more palatable than the idea that there is no final answer; or that the 'global elite', rather than possessing ultimate knowledge, may be as confused and conflicted as everyone else (although they are probably having a much more comfortable pandemic).

Much like indoctrination into a cult, the intricate, esoteric business of becoming an initiate is also appealing. Conspiracy theories encourage the belief that you are heroically navigating a maze of clandestine knowledge towards the One True Explanation. Narratives like the 'deep state' paranoia of QAnon are fuelled in part by the game-like excitement of unearthing clues: of earning your place as an insider, complete with an insider's righteousness and entitlements. Opposing this kind of paranoid bad faith is one of rigorous thinking's great challenges – and evidence and reasoning are only part of the answer.[26]

Testing rival explanations

How can I be sure that the world isn't ruled by a shadowy elite, or that the entire universe isn't a computer simulation, or a dream, or a test created by super-advanced aliens? The answer is that I can't – but this is because all of these 'explanations' are formulated in a manner that makes them equally interchangeable. They explain everything, and thus they explain nothing. There are no facts or discoveries that can't be fitted into their circular logic.

⇨ Can you think of any examples of conspiracy theories you've come across?

⇨ Why do you think people choose to believe them?

⇨ What might it mean to successfully challenge them, or to open people's minds?

You might think this makes them easy to identify and dismiss. Yet perhaps the most troubling feature of conspiracy theories is that – although simpler explanations are inherently more plausible than complex ones (because they require fewer things to be true) – we can never definitively rule out any explanation purely on the basis of complexity. Indeed, conspiracy theories embody an extreme version of something we can all be guilty of: hanging on to a favoured interpretation of events with more tenacity than the evidence warrants.

The preference underlying this is called *confirmation bias*, and it describes the universal human tendency to seek confirmation of those things we already believe, or wish to be true, in preference to anything that contradicts these feelings or beliefs.[27] What is to be done? One answer relates to the themes with which this chapter began: building steel rather than straw men; and engaging as fully as possible with rival perspectives.

To see what this looks like in practice, consider a period of European history sometimes known as the Enlightenment. In the early 17th century, astronomers found themselves struggling to reconcile their increasingly accurate observations of the night sky with the (widespread but incorrect) belief that the planets *must* move in circular orbits, circles being perfect manifestations of divine order.

It wasn't until Johannes Kepler published his treatises on the laws of planetary motion, between 1609 and 1619, that the planets' actual, elliptical orbits were first mathematically described. Yet Kepler's own work originated in a religiously inspired determination to prove that these orbits were circular. How did he end up changing his mind?

Kepler's first book set out an intricate geometrical scheme describing circles as the basis for all creation. When, however, he inherited the astronomical observations of his mentor, Tycho Brahe, in 1601, he decided to use these not just to bolster his existing theories but also – crucially – to put them to a *test*. Brahe possessed extraordinarily detailed observations of Mars's orbit. And it was by comparing these records to his theory's best predictions that Kepler gradually realized that the mathematics of circles could not explain what had been observed; but that, if these circles were flattened into ellipses with the Sun located at one of their two foci, everything fell into place.

Kepler continued to believe that this evidenced a divine plan for creation (and spent much of his professional life dispensing astrological advice). What he also did, however, was embrace two further principles that underpinned many of his age's insights:

- Human understanding, although it may be divinely inspired, should nevertheless be guided by the exploration and measurement of the universe, rather than just by the interpretation of scriptural and classical authorities.
- The descriptive and predictive power of even a highly favoured explanation could and should be tested against potentially superior alternatives.

At this point, it's worth mentioning one of the most important 20th-century thinkers to have written about scientific explanations: the philosopher Karl Popper. Popper was acutely aware of both the tumultuous history of scientific thought and the ongoing challenges posed to clear thinking by confirmation bias. Rather than despair at the impossibility of explaining anything with absolute certainty, however, Popper realised that the history of science pointed to a profoundly significant asymmetry between *verification* and *falsification*. His reasoning went like this:

i If you only seek confirmation, it's possible endlessly to find evidence that supports anything you might wish to believe, no matter how unlikely or implausible it is.
ii This means that we can't be sure that any claim is absolutely correct on the basis of even seemingly overwhelming

confirmatory evidence. Similarly, any favoured idea or explanation can be 'saved' by sufficiently complex additions.

iii We can, however, seek out evidence that decisively demonstrates some types of claim to be false. If, for example, I claim that there are no snakes in North America, then finding just one snake in North America is enough to disprove this claim.

iv Similarly, even when absolute disproof is impossible, we can come up with investigations that establish how *likely* a claim is to be false. If I'm investigating whether a new vaccine protects against a disease and discover that, in a well-controlled experiment, 997 out of 1,000 vaccinated people gain immunity, I know that the likelihood of such a result occurring simply by chance is vanishingly low when compared to the likelihood that the vaccine has had an effect.

v Despite the absence of certainty, we can thus achieve progress in our understanding of the world by coming up with claims that meaningfully and specifically invite falsification – or that allow us to test their plausibility to a high degree of confidence.

REFLECTION BOX 5.3

⇨ What is a topic you might wish to investigate or understand more about?

⇨ What is your current understanding of this area?

⇨ How might you formulate a working explanation or theory to help you test and improve your understanding?

Although much is made of the 'scientific method', it's perhaps more accurate to think of scientific research as a family of interconnected attitudes and approaches, practised within a variety of contexts by researchers who are themselves only too human.

Similarly, it's possible to take Popper's account of falsification too far and to overlook the fundamentally imaginative, cultural and creative leaps underpinning many of science's great insights.

Kepler didn't simply stumble upon some data he couldn't explain and, as a result, transform his thinking. He lived at a historical moment when numerous astronomers were wrestling with the implications of increasingly accurate telescopic observations and with the practical challenge of producing reliable astronomical charts and navigation aids. There are, however, some general questions that – after Popper – we can apply to many occasions upon which rigorous explanations are being sought:

  i What is it that we are interested in exploring and understanding?
 ii What does our current explanation propose is going on?
iii Are there observations that are incompatible with our explanation? What predictions might we make to enable us to test our explanation?
 iv If either of the above produces results incompatible with our explanation, is there a different explanation that can better account for everything we now know?
  v If everything we know and predict does turn out to be compatible with our explanation, is this also true of any other, simpler explanation?
 vi If our explanation both explains everything and is the simplest we can find, how might we test it still more rigorously, and improve its power and precision?

Notice that there is no final bullet point saying: 'Stop, you have discovered the ultimate truth!' There is only the business of seeking to explain more, about which the most important thing we can say is always this:

> In the light of our current knowledge, this explanation is better than the rest, because it offers the richest and most precise insights and predictions.

Let's turn to the present moment to see how everything hangs together. In the earliest days of the pandemic – in January and early February 2020, when it was still being treated as a viral outbreak local to China – one prevalent theory was that the virus had a very low transmission rate between people. Animal-to-human contact was seen as the main source of infection. Human-to-human transmission was assumed to be unlikely, as is often the case with novel diseases that are adapted to animal rather than human hosts. As the pandemic progressed, the six questions outlined above played out something like this:

i *What are we interested in?* We are interested in exploring and understanding how the novel coronavirus recently observed in China is spread.

ii *What is our current understanding?* Our best current explanation of its initial spread is that it is almost exclusively transmitted between animals and humans.

iii *What do we know, and what do we need to know to test this understanding?* There is some limited, early evidence emerging of possible human-to-human transmission. Our current explanation predicts a very low level of human-to-human transmission. Anything higher than this low level would thus suggest that this explanation is incorrect or, at best, flawed.

iv *Should we now be actively seeking an alternative explanation?* As events move forward, with the virus now spreading beyond China, we have found increasingly credible evidence of human-to-human transmission, making it likely that we need to treat this as a virus that is actually readily transmissible between humans.

v *What is the simplest new explanation able to account for what we now know?* Our new explanation is that the virus is transmissible between humans via virus-containing droplets of sweat, snot and saliva that may contaminate surfaces, or be spread through the air over short distances via coughing, sneezing and speech.

vi *How can we continue to test and improve our understanding?* As we continue to test our working explanations against the global spread of the virus, we are beginning to believe that droplets alone cannot account for what we are seeing, and that we also need to consider 'aerosol' spread as an explanation, entailing smaller particles that can remain suspended in exhaled air for several hours. We are continuing to refine our understanding by assessing the impacts of preventative measures such as social distancing and mask-wearing, alongside the analysis of so-called 'superspreading' events, which data suggests are responsible for many new infections.

Perhaps the most important point about this synopsis is that it doesn't contain any kind of *eureka!* moment. It embodies, rather, the collective activities of the global scientific community in advancing and exploring different, imperfect explanations in the light of incrementally improving knowledge.

As I type these words, it's 14 July 2020. Global deaths have passed half a million; confirmed cases have passed 13 million; in nations such as the USA, Mexico, Brazil, India, Russia and Peru, the virus continues to spread at a frightening rate. At the same time, countless minor explanations and ideas are gradually being tested and falsified – or judged robust enough to be further tested or implemented.

Above and beyond our growing understanding of how the virus spreads, an increasing number of trials suggest that the use of old drugs in new ways (in particular, the anti-viral Remdesivir and the steroid Dexamethasone) can significantly improve the survival rate of severely ill patients. Meanwhile, headline-grabbing early trials into the anti-malarial drug hydroxychloroquine have (in the best Popperian style) been shown to be unconvincing by subsequent investigations, despite its opportunistic touting by some politicians.

Much continues to change. The existence of an alarming variety of post-COVID-19 syndromes and symptoms is becoming apparent, and increasingly closely monitored, alongside potential new variants of the virus. As my potted synopsis suggests, the WHO is shifting its focus away from droplet transmission towards the analysis and prevention of airborne transmission: a change that, like any scientific rethink, is cautiously to be celebrated even while it throws up further public health and political challenges. Nothing about COVID-19 is perfectly understood or explicable; but our ignorance and impotence are, falteringly, being lessened, at least in the scientific domain.

Most significantly, there may, by the time you read this, be such a thing as effective vaccinations against the virus. There is no certainty here, and its absence continues to bring anger, controversy and heartbreak. But there is indubitably progress, as measured by the incremental advance of interconnected observations, analyses and attempted explanations – and by the abandoned and refuted ideas littering the path behind us. As Popper put it in his 1959 book *The Logic of Scientific Discovery*:

It is not truisms which science unveils. Rather, it is part of the greatness and the beauty of science that we can learn, through our own critical investigations, that the world is utterly different from what we ever imagined – until our imagination was fired by the refutation of our earlier theories.[28]

Summary and recommendations

- Constructing an over-simplified version of someone else's point of view just so that you can dismiss it is called *building a straw man.*
- Try instead to *build a steel man:* to engage with the strongest possible version of others' arguments.
- This echoes the *principle of charity*, which suggests you should attempt to extract the maximum possible truthful and reasonable content from what others say.
- A *good explanation* should account for all the relevant information you know while being as simple as possible. A *bad explanation* tends to ignore inconvenient information, or introduce unnecessary complexities.
- The simplest explanation isn't always the best. But complexity generally needs to be justified rather than assumed.
- It is possible endlessly to *confirm* anything you wish to believe if all you do is look for examples that support it.
- Wherever possible, seek *falsification* over confirmation; and don't be seduced by a theory that it's impossible to disprove. To explain everything is to explain nothing.
- The *scientific method* aspires to make predictions on the basis of a theory. If empirical observations prove incompatible with this theory, it then seeks either a new theory, a new interpretation, or some good explanation for these anomalies.
- Scientific thinking is interested in seeking the best possible explanation in the light of current knowledge – something that demands an ongoing, rigorous competition between rival theories.

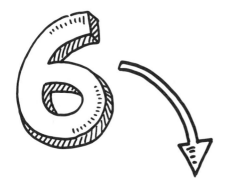

Creative and collaborative thinking: Finding a process that works

⇨ Imagination and creativity

⇨ Overcoming obstacles and developing original ideas

⇨ Building better collaborations

Imagination and creativity

I ended the previous chapter with Popper's description of the scientific imagination being 'fired' by the refutation of previous theories. This may seem an unusual way of describing science if you're used to treating it as a cool, emotionless discipline. Yet – as this chapter explores – imagination and creativity are just as integral to the sciences as to the arts; and just as amenable to active cultivation.

What is the difference between imagination and creativity? In everyday speech, these two words often describe similar things: free-flowing, associative forms of thinking that conjure up fresh possibilities; that entail sparks of inspiration and insight; that may be driven by or evoke deep feelings. Tapping into your imagination tends to be treated as a synonym for being creative, in the sense of stepping outside of everyday constraints.

There is also, however, an important distinction between them. Creativity is the *application* of imagination. We *imagine* things within the privacy and comfort of our minds: within a space where anything and everything is possible. But channelling this imagination into creativity means bringing something into existence: an artwork, an idea, a song, a scientific theory. However natural or spontaneous, creativity implies some form of craft or practice – and it is thus something that can be taught and refined.

In his 2001 book *Out of Our Minds: Learning to be Creative*, the British educationalist Sir Ken Robinson draws a distinction between imagination, creativity and a third concept, innovation:

> There are three related ideas … *imagination*, which is the process of bringing to mind things that are not present to our senses; *creativity*, which is the process of developing original ideas that have value; and *innovation*, which is the process of putting new ideas into practice.[29]

Plenty of other definitions exist, but Robinson is eloquent when it comes to treating creativity as a key aspect of learning (as opposed to a luxury or an indulgence) and locating it alongside innovation's promise to transform what we think and do. Do you agree with his framing? Before we go any further, consider the questions in Reflection Box 6.1.

⇨ What does creativity mean to you – and what part do you feel it plays in your life?

⇨ How do you feel creativity differs between the contexts of study, work and leisure?

⇨ How might you seek to practise and cultivate your creativity?

One of the trickiest things about discussing creativity is its personal, subjective nature. If I claim that whatever I'm doing is creative, who are you to contradict me? Or, if I feel that creativity isn't something I'm capable of, what does it matter if you feel differently? For some people, the idea of teaching creativity might seem inherently redundant. You are either a 'creative' person or you aren't.

I don't agree with these views – but I can see why some people hold them. For young children, creativity is inherent in play and learning. Children are innately inclined towards what is sometimes termed *divergent thinking*, which entails the free-flowing generation of different ideas. By contrast, it takes time and practice to develop *convergent thinking*, in which one particular idea is developed while others are discarded. Teaching convergent thinking is one of the primary tasks of education, and this makes it easy to see divergent thinking as a 'natural' attribute that people simply possess to varying, innate degrees.

The problem with this mindset is that it associates only divergent thinking with creativity, while assuming that only convergent thinking can be taught. This brings us to the importance of *unlearning* a number of faulty assumptions:

- Creativity isn't just about artistic acts, or only undertaken by 'creative' people. Any task that entails the exercise of judgement and skill has some creative element to it.
- Creative thinking doesn't have to be big, bold or strikingly original. It most often involves modest, everyday things:

conducting a lively conversation; coming up with a fresh angle on a familiar question.

- Creativity is not so much a single, spontaneous act as a process. It is something that can be learned, taught and practised, and encompasses convergent and divergent ways of thinking.

This last point is the most important of all. It is only too easy to be paralysed by the belief that creativity is an all-or-nothing business: that an original, creative inspiration either arrives out of the blue, or doesn't. In fact, the opposite is far closer to the truth. The more someone relies upon creative thinking in their day-to-day life, the more likely they are also to rely upon a step-by-step process to help and support them. Here is the American author and Nobel laureate Toni Morrison discussing her creative process in a 2014 interview:

> As a writer, a failure is just information. It's something that I've done wrong in writing, or is inaccurate or unclear. I recognize failure – which is important; some people don't – and fix it, because it is data, it is information, knowledge of what does not work ... It's as though you're in a laboratory and you're working on an experiment with chemicals or with rats, and it doesn't work. It doesn't mix. You don't throw up your hands and run out of the lab. What you do is you identify the procedure and what went wrong and then correct it.[30]

Morrison's words are at once remarkable and salutary in their alignment of literary creativity with the language of scientific research: *information, data, laboratory, experiment, procedure.* She produced some of the most eloquent and profound accounts of African American experience ever committed to prose. Yet, in this instance, she chose to frame her creativity in terms of information being meticulously analysed; of a repeatedly refined experiment. She chose, in other words, to foreground the fact that underlying even the greatest creative works is a structured process, full of false steps and necessary corrections.

What can we usefully generalize about such processes? In recent years, one modern take has been pioneered by the anthropologist and artist Eitan Buchalter, with whom I've been fortunate to collaborate on its applications in education. Buchalter's approach has the merit – in my opinion – of being at once practical and sufficiently open-ended to be applicable from primary schools to universities. It breaks the creative process down into six steps:

i *Interests*: First, you identify through reflection and imagination an area of interest: one that speaks to you on a deep, intuitive level.

ii *Knowledge*: You reflect upon what you already know about this subject; what is special and surprising about it; what knowledge, skills and experience you bring.

iii *Play*: Governed by the question of what it means to convey your interest to others, you playfully experiment, testing out what you might make and do.

iv *Findings*: You record and reflect upon your experiments: the challenges you found; how these might be overcome; what you might change or adapt.

v *Context*: You research what other work has been done in this area; what it achieved and how; and what lessons and questions are most relevant to you.

vi *Feedback*: You reflect upon what you have done and learned; how you feel about it; and what it might mean to make it better. Then, as necessary, you repeat all six steps.[31]

How does this relate to your own experiences? As you may have noticed, the six steps that Buchalter proposes move between invitations to open-ended experimentation and focused reflection, deploying these in sequence to widen and then narrow your focus. Far from being rival modes that risk cancelling each other out, this movement between divergent and convergent attitudes is characteristic of creativity as Morrison and many others describe it, with both its gusts of inspiration and its painstaking self-reflections.

Most importantly, when it comes to teaching and learning, *being able to undertake such a process* is itself the key lesson for creativity. This, Buchalter emphasizes, contrasts with the intense focus on craft skills often found in classrooms, where those with a certain level of aptitude or expertise are likely to thrive while others end up classifying themselves as 'uncreative'. In other words:

- Intuition and critical reflection go hand in hand within a successful creative process, which entails moving between divergent and convergent modes of thinking.
- It's important to distinguish *craft* from creativity. Particular craft skills may be necessary for creating certain things, but these skills aren't 'creative' in themselves.
- Learning to engage in a meaningful creative process is *itself* the key transferable lesson when it comes to teaching and practising creativity.
- Being able to engage in such a process is valuable not just for an artistic few, but for everyone – with its applications extending far beyond the arts.

How might you make use of such a process yourself? Consider the questions in Reflection Box 6.2.

REFLECTION BOX 6.2

⇨ What would it most excite you to address or explore in an original project of your own?

⇨ How might you bring creativity to bear on one, small aspect of your current work?

⇨ What have you done, in the past, that you feel embodies successful creative thinking?

Overcoming obstacles and developing original ideas

Whether you're contemplating a research project, a dissertation or a professional challenge, it's easy to be paralysed by the question of *how to begin* – and by anxiety over what an adequately original, interesting or innovative approach might be. Here's one piece of advice it's worth taking to heart in response to these inhibitions:

Originality, interest and innovation are *not* about ground-breaking novelty. Much of the time, they simply mean finding a new angle from which to explore an existing question; or using a different method to resolve a familiar issue; or bringing a personal, reflective approach to an existing debate. Never aspire to novelty for its own sake.

At this point, a confession. I write textbooks and non-fiction, but I am also a novelist. At least, I have published one novel: a thriller written in parallel with my recent non-fiction. And perhaps the most important lesson I needed to take on board in order to write it was rooted in *unlearning* an unhelpful cliché: everyone has a novel inside them.

You might think of this as an inspiring claim. For me, however, the problem was simple: it suggested that writing a novel meant looking inside me and somehow finding a novel's essence, waiting to be written. I didn't have anything like this inside me. So, for years, I did nothing about it.

Eventually, a series of conversations and opportunities inspired me to make a start, even though I didn't have a perfect plot or roster of characters raring to go. I began writing, introduced a character and a scene, then worried away at what might happen next. I rewrote everything, added another scene, introduced another character. I changed the gender of my first character, thought of another scene, found myself inspired by a friend's recent book about the dark side of the internet, re-read and rewrote everything again, and added another scene. Gradually I found that, despite my uncertainties and insecurities, I was indeed writing a novel.

I didn't yet know how its story would end, or whether it would be any good. But I no longer worried about whether it was possible, or whether I could come up with a sufficiently grand, original concept. I had committed to a creative process and, by doing so, had escaped the trap of assuming novels were somehow natural and innate. They were, I realized, remarkably similar to the non-fiction I'd already written, in the sense that – so long as I stuck with a rigorous enough process – a book would be the end result.

Is it self-indulgent of me to talk about my own experiences? Quite possibly. They're certainly not universal. Some authors *do* feel as though they have novels inside them, waiting to be written.

Plenty plan their plots meticulously in advance. Some barely revise what they're writing – or do so all at once, after the first draft is done. Some write religiously between certain hours, or produce an exact number of words per day. Others write all night, or only at the weekend. Some go on rural retreats. Others pour out their words around the exhausted edges of work and childcare. Yet all of them have one thing in common: they find a way to fill the first blank page, then to keep going until the work is done.

This is the only guarantee when it comes to any undertaking, creative or otherwise. You need to find a way to get the work done, and this means finding a process that *works for you*: that allows you to overcome whatever is inhibiting your imagination and execution. What might this mean for you? Consider the questions in Reflection Box 6.3.

REFLECTION BOX 6.3

⇨ What are your most significant blocks and inhibitions when it comes to starting a project?

⇨ In what ways might you give yourself permission to make a start?

⇨ What are your most significant blocks and inhibitions when it comes to keeping going?

⇨ What might a process that you could commit to, day after day, look and feel like?

These questions invite you to explore the obstacles standing between you and your aspirations. They're more likely to be useful if you can answer them specifically; that is, by reflecting upon immediate, practical issues rather than abstract ones. You may fear failure, but it's hard to do something about this unless you break this fear down into particular elements. One obstacle may be, say, the fear of looking foolish in front of certain people; or the fact that you find a key resource difficult or dull. These suggest, respectively, that you should explore why particular people intimidate you and where you might look for support; or that seeking out some new resources better suited to your preferences may be useful.

I sometimes mentor other writers, and one common framework for conducting a mentoring session can be useful for working through such challenges:

i *Set yourself a practical goal.* What do you want to achieve? Where do you want to be in a month's time and in a year's time? Once you have set out some positive, concrete goals, you can start thinking about timings and next steps.

ii *Consider the realities of your situation.* What is happening for you, right now? What are your main stumbling blocks and challenges? What are your assets and skills?

iii *Set out your options.* Given your situation, what are your immediate options? What tools, opportunities and connections are available to you? Can you break down what needs to happen into small, achievable steps?

iv *Decide what you will go and do.* Having looked at what you *could* do, you now need to decide what you are *actually* going to go and do. If possible, set time-specific commitments. These can be very small: the important thing is to end up with a commitment to some particular, immediate action.

It's also useful to beware of one hazard that can stand in the way of starting and sustaining any project, whether or not you believe it to be a 'creative' one: making the perfect the enemy of the good.

To make the perfect the enemy of the good is to decline to attempt something on the grounds that the result will be imperfect, even if there might have been plenty of good things about it. Someone who doesn't feel able to keep going because they don't feel sufficiently talented or experienced is suffering from a version of this problem – as is someone too concerned about sounding foolish to speak up in a seminar or meeting, or too preoccupied with potential criticisms to contribute to a debate.

It's a situation almost all of us will have experienced at some point in our lives, and overcoming it brings us to the second half of this chapter's title: collaborative thinking, and its close connections to creativity.

Building better collaborations

What are the most important ingredients in a successful collaboration? Three factors in particular recur as a common ground. These are:

- *Successful communication*: creating conditions within which people can clearly explain themselves, are able to grasp others' perspectives, and everyone is heard without one voice dominating.
- *Common values*: establishing shared goals and understandings of what the task at hand is about, its scope and underlying principles; and of what constitutes respectful, inclusive conduct.
- *Iteration*: ensuring regular, constructive assessments of an undertaking's outputs; and improving and refining these outputs alongside current objectives and priorities.

As you may have noticed, these echo several of the principles set out in my previous chapters about assumptions and reasoning. How, though, do they connect to what I've said so far about creativity?

Most importantly, they are about a process that embraces trying, and trying again, rather than aiming at perfection; that relies by its very nature on constructive feedback, and on each participant's ability to embrace this alongside incremental improvement; and that creates spaces within which divergent views can be cultivated, and collective lessons drawn from reflecting upon them.

To collaborate meaningfully is to draw insights from a diversity of perspectives gathered around a common cause: to embrace the interactions between divergence and convergence. It's also, contrary to some models of leadership, to shun the stifling of creativity that comes from micro-management – and from privileging public performances of 'innovative thinking' over the meticulous labour of genuine creativity.

In the 2004 book *On Film-Making*, which gathers the director Alexander Mackendrick's teachings on the inherently collaborative art of film-making, Mackendrick addresses the importance of this labour when it comes to connecting imagination and creativity:

One of the things I find most frequently missing in students … is not imagination itself, [but] rather the knack of making a disciplined effort in the development of fertile imagination … People who talk about things instead of doing them tend to use analysis as a substitute for creativity. But a statement about the kind of effect you want to achieve is never a substitute for the often exhausting labours that must go into actually creating that effect. Work is the only real training.[32]

If you wish to produce meaningful work, you must first acquire the habit simply of producing work – which, through its successes and failures, will teach you what it means to fail, next time, a little less. Similarly, any successful collaboration needs to embrace the imperfections of successive efforts and inputs as the preconditions of purposeful iteration. Consider the questions in Reflection Box 6.4.

REFLECTION BOX 6.4

⇨ How do you feel about sharing your own work with others?

⇨ What kind of feedback do you appreciate most – or worry about?

⇨ How would you set about giving someone else meaningful, constructive feedback?

The questions above are staples of coaching, counselling and facilitation: processes intended to help deepen and clarify people's sense of what matters, and why; and to offer opportunities for constructive reflection and iteration. In particular, a technique known as *active listening* is often used in such settings, and has several components:

- *Attending* closely to what someone else is saying – and showing you are doing so through posture, eye contact and non-verbal signals such as smiling and nodding.
- *Allowing* someone else to speak rather than interrupting, while focusing on trying to understand them as fully as possible rather than trying to fill every silence.

- *Asking* specific questions to clarify your understanding if you are confused; or prompting someone to expand on their ideas with open-ended questions.
- *Summarizing* your understanding of what someone has told you, once they have finished speaking, and allowing them to correct and update your summary as needed.

Taken together, these techniques can be a powerful way of engaging deeply with other people's positions. They invite you to embrace rather than shudder at reflection and feedback, and to extend this invitation to others.[33] Especially in the context of online interactions, this kind of openness and attentiveness is vital to successful communication. In particular:

- Asking someone to clarify their thoughts, feelings or assumptions with an open question can pay great dividends in contexts where intentions can be difficult to interpret, such as remote meetings.
- A blend of different communication techniques can be extremely effective at getting the most out of a group. Consider using a mixture of *synchronous* (interacting simultaneously in real time, like an in-person conversation or live chat) and *asynchronous* (making contributions at different times, such as via email, shared documents or social media groups) contexts to include those with different preferences.
- Try to emphasize not only *common goals* and *common values*, but also *constructive critiques,* which focus not so much on saying 'here's what is wrong with your contribution' as 'here are some of the ways I think we could make this *better*'.

Strange though it may seem, it's important not to take things too personally when it comes to both creativity and collaboration. A verdict on something you've offered or made is not a verdict on *you*, even if it purports to be. And once you've learned not to take such things personally, you become free to treat them as information, to be put to work however best serves your aims.

Ultimately, all creative artefacts must stand or fall not by the intentions behind them, but by their effects upon a particular audience.

This encounter may feel frightening, unfair or arbitrary (and it can be all of these things), but it's also a great equalizer. No matter how successful or talented they may be, nobody can control the reception of their work. The only guarantee is that those who don't create something will never reap the rewards of doing so; and that, given a good enough process, we can all hope to play a part in bringing something worthwhile to fruition.

Summary and recommendations

- *Imagination* is a personal and private act of invention. *Creativity* is the application of imagination, and can thus be taught and refined.
- Don't treat creativity as something people either naturally have, or don't. Treat it as a deliberate process, open to all.
- *Divergent thinking* entails the free-flowing generation of varied ideas and possibilities, while *convergent thinking* means focusing upon and developing one particular idea while discarding others.
- A successful *creative process* moves between both these modes of thinking, cultivating times and spaces that enable each in turn.
- Eitan Buchalter's six-step model offers a practical example of one such process, moving from identifying *Interests* to reflecting upon *Knowledge*, then to experimental *Play* and a recording of *Findings*, then to researching *Context* and reflective *Feedback*.
- Don't confuse *craft* with creativity, and don't assume creative thinking applies only to art. It underpins everything from scientific research to institutional leadership.
- Don't be paralysed by the thought that creative work must be *original* or groundbreaking. There is no such thing as perfect originality. A single question, insight, variation or fresh perspective can be a meaningful creative contribution.
- Successful collaborations share a common ground with successful creative processes in their capacity for embracing *imperfections*, *feedback* and *iteration*.
- To collaborate meaningfully is to draw as much benefit as possible from a diversity of perspectives gathered around a common cause.

- *Active listening* embodies a powerful set of techniques for more deeply engaging with others' positions, and for exploring your own.
- Many valuable lessons can only be learned by embarking upon the work itself. Perhaps the only guarantee with any undertaking is that you need to find a way to overcome whatever is inhibiting you, to begin – and then to keep going.

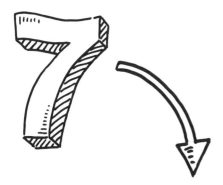

Thinking about numbers: How not to lie with statistics

⇨ Looking into the stories behind data

⇨ Identifying common misuses of statistics

⇨ Probability, variability and representation

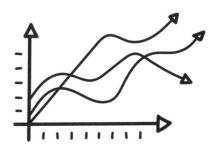

Looking into the stories behind data

All data is made, not found. And unless you have some awareness of the processes through which it's made, you're likely to fall into error.

Consider something as straightforward as the population of a country. As I type these words, it's 12:57 on Tuesday 14 July 2020. What is the population of my home country, the United Kingdom, right now? What I mean by this question is perfectly clear. The population of a country is usually defined as its total number of inhabitants – that is, the number of people who live there, as opposed to those who are just visiting. I want to know what this total is for the UK as of this exact moment.

It's a question for which a correct answer definitively exists. If I could somehow freeze time and mobilize a drone army to scan every inch of the country, I could theoretically determine this answer. Given that I can't, however, I'm instead going to type my query into a search engine, then click on a likely source for an accurate and up-to-date answer: the website of the UK Office for National Statistics (the ONS for short). Having done this, its most recent report tells me that the UK population is estimated at 66,796,807. Great! I have now found what I was looking for. Or have I?

Clearly, I haven't. For a start, the UK's population is likely to have changed even since I asked my question. During the five minutes I've been writing this chapter, it's likely that some people have been born and some have died. Further searches within the ONS website tell me that there were 721,685 live births in the UK over the most recent recorded year. During the same year, there were 593,410 registered deaths. Taken together, these imply a net annual gain of 128,275 humans: approximately 351.4 people every day, or 0.24 people per minute.

This is only on average, though, and it doesn't take into account immigration and emigration, which are estimated over the same period to have been 609,308 and 378,774 respectively, yielding a net gain of 230,534 people – around 631.6 per day, or another 0.44 people per minute. Overall, then, it seems every minute sees an average of 0.68 new human inhabitants of the UK. That's 3.4 in the last five minutes!

Am I getting closer to some kind of truth or understanding? Not really. Leaving aside the absurdity of translating annual changes into minute-by-minute fractions of humans, I haven't begun to engage with two important questions: *when* the figure of 66,796,807 refers to, and *how* it was arrived at. Given all of the factors noted above, it can hardly be exact – but it looks awfully precise for an estimate. What's going on?

The ONS website informs me that this figure was released on 24 June 2020, and that it is an estimate of the UK's population in June 2019. That's just over a year ago, as I write this chapter – but it's also the most recent detailed information available. How did the ONS arrive at the figure? Here's part of its official account:

> The resident population, by single year of age, on 30 June of the year prior to the reference year is aged by one year [i.e. they take the previous year's figures for the UK population and add one year to the recorded age of each person], those born during the 12-month period prior to the mid-year point are added on to the population and those who have died during the 12-month period are removed … Other factors taken into account are the movement of people into and out of the UK (international migration) and movements between areas of the UK (internal migration) … Some population sub-groups such as prisoners and armed forces (UK and foreign) are estimated separately from the rest of the population.

This is probably more detail than you or I ever wanted to know about population estimates. I started off looking for a figure for the UK's current population. I've now ended up with what appears to be a pretty good figure for its population 13 months ago, plus lots of detail about how this was calculated. Is there any way I can update this myself? Between mid-2018 and mid-2019, the ONS tells me that the UK's population increased from 66,435,550 to 66,796,807 – an increase of 0.54%. If I assume that it also increased by around 0.5% over the next year, this means that it may by now be more like 67,100,000, to the nearest 100,000.

Phew. I now have a rough estimate of the UK's current population. It's not exact, but it's more than enough to satisfy idle curiosity – and little different from the first thing that came up when I typed in my query online. Why, then, should I care about any of the details above? Is any of it relevant to any situation beyond a research project into population statistics?

The answer is that, much of the time, it's not. Having some understanding of how statistics are arrived at can, however, become very significant when it comes to making and assessing claims about what they *mean* – and what it is, and isn't, reasonable to infer based upon them. To see why, take a look at Table 7.1. It contains the complete data from the ONS website, followed by five statistical claims and some questions about them (the latter in Reflection Box 7.1):

Table 7.1   Components of UK population change

	Mid-2019	**Mid-2018**	**5-year average**
Births	721,685	743,933	756,862
Deaths	593,410	622,944	602,116
Natural change (births minus deaths)	128,275	120,989	154,746
International immigration	609,318	625,927	618,517
International emigration	378,804	350,934	337,230
Net international migration	230,514	274,993	281,291
Other changes	2,467	–683	3,973
Total change	361,257	395,321	440,011
% change	0.54	0.60	0.67

Source: Office for National Statistics, National Records of Scotland, Northern Ireland Statistics and Research Agency – Population Estimates

i This year, there are around 361,000 more people in the UK than there were last year; this must tell us how many more people were born than died.

ii Over 609,000 immigrants came to the UK in the most recent year they've got figures for. Meanwhile, there were only 128,000 more births than deaths. That's almost half a million more immigrants than native births! Within a few decades, immigrants will be in the majority.

iii Did you know that, every single day in the UK, 1,626 people die – and 1,038 people leave the country?

iv Every year, the UK population increases by around half a per cent. It's 66,796,807 million today, so by 2030 it will be 70,212,804.

v   More of the UK's population growth is due to immigration than to births.

// REFLECTION BOX 7.1

⇨ How far do you find each of these five claims reasonable or convincing?

⇨ How might someone react to the claims above if they didn't know anything about the underlying statistics in question?

⇨ Do they represent an accurate analysis based on the ONS statistics – or do they distort or misrepresent them?

///

As you may have guessed, not one of the above claims is entirely accurate – and several are either false or significantly misleading. Here is my analysis of each:

i   This first claim is simply wrong: the increase in the UK population isn't the same thing as births minus deaths, because it also needs to include immigration minus emigration (the UK's population increase of 361,257 includes the 230,514 difference between immigration and emigration).

ii This claim is both wrong and highly misleading. While 609,318 people did immigrate to the UK, 378,804 also emigrated – and we'd need to find out what proportion of each number represents leaving or returning 'natives' to say anything about long-term trends. Similarly, there were 721,685 births in the UK and 593,410 deaths – and, again, we don't know what proportion of each of these entails 'natives'. The term 'native' is itself undefined, confusing and loaded with unhelpful racial overtones. Moreover, the maths of the original claim is faulty; it would take more than 'a few decades' for an annual change of half a million people a year to constitute a majority. We'd also need to investigate the existing composition of the UK population, and of those migrating and emigrating, to meaningfully analyse such changes.

iii These daily numbers do represent an accurate average – but they aren't, as implied, precise numbers for something that happens 'every day', and to say so is misleading. Both death rates and emigration timings vary considerably during the course of the year. Moreover, in the absence of the context of birth and immigration rates, there's the risk that this claim could implicitly be read as evidence for the (inaccurate) claim that the UK population is shrinking.

iv This extrapolation of an approximate rate of growth over the next decade is not wholly unreasonable – but the degree of precision it supplies is. Offering a precise number for a country's population ten years into the future is misleading, because nothing like this degree of accuracy is possible. It would be better to say something like, 'in a decade's time the UK population is likely to be around 70 million, if current trends continue'. Also, the original data in question actually refers to mid-2019, making ten years ahead of it 2029, not 2030.

v This statement is almost accurate – but it's also potentially misleading. The problem is that, although most of the UK's recent population increase is in one sense the result of migration, there are nevertheless more births per year in the UK than there are people immigrating – but this is outweighed by the fact that many more people die than emigrate. We can better capture this by saying that 'net international migration' (immigration minus emigration) causes more of the UK's population growth than 'natural change' (births minus deaths).

How did your analyses compare to mine? Did you find yourself taking any of the five statements at face value? If so, have you now changed your mind?[34]

Identifying common misuses of statistics

The words 'data' and 'statistics' are sometimes used interchangeably, but it's more useful to think of data as raw informational material, and statistics as the result of the processing and analysis of this material. First, data is created by observation or measurement. Next, this data is processed and/or contextualised to produce statistical claims – something that both adapts it to a particular purpose and, potentially, embeds a host of assumptions within it.

When it comes to population estimates, for example, the previous section didn't even touch on the most crucial and contentious element of all: creating raw data via a census. In the UK, a census is conducted once a decade, and entails sending out a detailed survey that every household in the country is legally obliged to complete. The result allows population estimates (and details such as occupations, ethnicity and age) to be updated against real-world measurements. But it's important to remember that even the most meticulous census is an imperfect measure, and one likely (for example) to under-count people who may be unable or reluctant to provide responses, such as undocumented immigrants.

In general, the most rigorous and useful statistics are handled in a way that mitigates against abuse and misunderstanding; that actively spells out absences and uncertainties present in the raw data; and that cleans up potential errors. This is why the ONS conducts both a Census Coverage Survey and a Census Quality Survey in addition to the main UK census. These entail re-surveying a carefully selected sample of the overall population to assess the extent and distribution of undercounting, and the likely error level in responses. For every such undertaking, however, there are dozens of misleading or misrepresented statistics to be guarded against.

As Mark Twain famously noted in his 1907 *Chapters from My Autobiography*, 'There are three kinds of lies: lies, damned lies, and statistics.' Statistics are the worst kind of lie, Twain mischievously suggests, because they masquerade as objective truths. It's only too easy for people to pretend that numbers are an impartial measure of the world while using them as anything but. Consider the questions in Reflection Box 7.2.

REFLECTION BOX 7.2

⇨ Can you think of a case of statistical deception that you've come across?

⇨ Why was this deception in particular being practised?

⇨ What might be a more accurate, honest way of discussing this particular statistic?

Similarly to other forms of fallacious or confused thinking, unreliable statistical claims are most likely to occur in contexts when people care more about 'winning' than describing what is actually going on – or when they ignore important uncertainties and complexities. In particular, it's worth watching out for these warning signs:

- Phrases like 'up to' or 'as much as', which suggest someone is using the top end of a range for maximum emotional impact, even though the range of possibilities is what's relevant. For example, an investment that claims 'up to 50% annual returns' isn't actually guaranteeing any return at all.
- Saying 'as little as' or 'from...' does the same for the lower end of a range: 'prices from one pound!' might mean only one item among thousands costs that little.
- Focusing exclusively on one element of a phenomenon that needs to be seen as a whole: discussing birth rates, say, as if they can on their own describe population change.
- Using spurious precision to create a bogus debate: statistics like economic growth are often discussed in minute detail, even though the data on which they're based isn't accurate enough for single fractions of a per cent to be meaningful.
- Comparing two different things as if they were equivalent, or as if there were a simple causal link between them. For example, household debt and national debt are unrelated, measured in different ways and not analogous, yet politicians frequently compare them in order to score rhetorical points.
- Using misleading visualizations, such as graphs that don't start at zero on each axis, or icons whose areas aren't proportional to what they 'represent'.
- Bamboozling people with huge 'total' numbers like millions or billions, rather than breaking these down in a useful way. Increasing educational spending by millions sounds great, until you realize it corresponds to just a few thousand pounds per school.
- Misleadingly focusing on percentage changes rather than absolute changes, or vice versa. The number of smartphones in the world has, for example, gone up by over a million per cent in 20 years – but this tells us very little. It may, however, be

Thinking About Numbers

more useful to know that a country's GDP has increased by 2% than that it went up by a billion dollars because, taken on its own, we can't tell whether a billion dollars is a lot or a little in the context of GDP.

- Relying on decontextualized, striking statistics that have gone viral, especially on social media. Almost invariably, these are distortions, fabrications or (at best) highly partisan simplifications of a much more complicated story.

Despite all this – and for all the torrents of misleading information that flow across our screens – the resources available at our fingertips also mean that it has never been easier to dispel some of this obfuscation, at least in theory. All you need to do is start digging into what lies behind the numbers; or to seek out the work of someone trustworthy who has already done so.

We've seen that the UK Office of National Statistics both explains exactly what its statistics describe, and presents the methodology and context behind them. In other words, it is extremely *transparent* about what is going on behind the scenes; and this kind of transparency is a key property of trustworthy statistics. By contrast, the less transparent a particular statistical claim is – and the more difficult it is to test or replicate the analysis behind it – the more cautious you should be about accepting it at face value.

When numbers are presented without explanation or justification, we are left in much the same position as we are when contemplating an unsupported assertion: cut off from any meaningful assessment of their merit. More than with most other forms of reasoning, however, it can be challenging to assess the quality, accuracy and limitations of statistics.

This in turn means that statistical transparency needs to be carefully framed and contextualized in order to be genuinely useful. To borrow a formulation from the philosopher Onora O'Neill, transparency alone is not enough to help us – and may even be counter-productive if it involves dumps of decontextualized data. What's needed is *intelligent forms of openness*, governed by the principles that information provision should be:

- *Accessible* – easy to access.
- *Assessable* – allowing users to check its reliability.

- *Intelligible* – presented in a way that aids understanding.
- *Useable* – allowing people to make their own use of data.

Taken together, these offer a practical guide to promoting better-informed public discussions of statistics. As O'Neill put it in her 2002 Reith lecture 'A Question of Trust':

> Global transparency and complete openness are not the best ways to build or restore trust. We place and refuse trust not because we have torrents of information (more is not always better), but because we can trace specific bits of information and specific undertakings to particular sources on whose veracity and reliability we can run some checks. Well-placed trust grows out of active inquiry rather than blind acceptance … So if we want a society in which placing trust is feasible we need to look for ways in which we can actively check one another's claims.[35]

Trustworthiness relies equally upon access to information and a reliable method for assessing this information, neither of which can be taken for granted in an age of effortlessly disseminated deception. In the end, it's our ability actively to engage with information, together – its provenance, its processing; the assumptions, values and blind spots it embodies – that defends its usefulness and integrity.

Probability, variability and representation

As O'Neill's formulation suggests, trust and reliability are bound up with *actively* interrogating claims and putting them to work. In general, useful and reliable statistics:

- Provide, based upon an *authoritative* or *reliable* source or method…
- …some acceptably *unambiguous* and *accurate* information…
- …that is *significant* and *relevant* in the context of…
- …something we *understand* and are *interested in analysing*.

For example, the result of a recent football game (by which I mean soccer, if you're reading this in the US) in the English Premier League is the kind of statistic that's so self-evidently reliable and self-explanatory that it may be strange to think of it as a statistic at all. It exhaustively describes the thing we're interested in; we can be confident it was recorded accurately; and its meaning is clear.

A slightly more complex example might be the number of passes made by team X during the game. This is a number that can in theory be checked by anyone with access to a recording. It's easy to define and discuss – but it is slightly harder to measure. A variety of companies generate football statistics, based on human observers totting up events in real time: attempts at goal, fouls, passes, tackles, assists, and so on. Counts can differ, thanks to human errors or differences in interpretation, but there's still a high degree of consensus around turning raw observational data into official statistics.

More complex again might be an attempt to measure the loyalty inspired by a club, based (say) on the average length of service of its players. Unlike goals or passes – which are defined, discrete events – a concept such as 'loyalty' isn't identical to a measure like 'the average length of time players have spent at a club'. Experts might argue that such an approach is too crude; that allowances need to be made for such things as youth academies, players who have left clubs and then returned, the length of service of coaches and managers, and so on. A statistic derived from data about players' length of service is thus far from meaningless – but what exactly it signifies is open to dispute.

Still more complex might be an effort to measure something such as 'the economic benefits of having a premier league football team to a town or city'. How could you set about assessing this? One way might be to look at all those places that have premier league clubs, and to compare their local economies to similar places that don't. Another might be to look at a particular place before and after it had a premier league club; yet another to try to quantify the total worth of different local economic activities boosted by or dependent upon football.

All of these suggestions are far from perfect, partly because it's so difficult to distinguish between *the effects of having a football club* and *the conditions that contribute to having one in the first place*. In general, questions like 'what are the economic benefits of X?' often assume too much in terms of X having particular, measurable effects. Unlike passes on a football field, you can't just employ a group of people to tot up the 'total economic effects that are entirely due to this place having a premier league football club'. All of which brings us to two points:

- All statistics fall short of the realities we're using them to discuss.
- A key question is thus how well we understand the gap between reality and its statistical description.

These points are encapsulated in the concept of *variability*, which describes the fact that, whenever we're trying to extract statistical insights from data, almost everything varies between different moments, places and cases. The UK population, for example, is constantly changing. So any population figure we come up with must be an estimated value for a particular point in time, based upon observations themselves limited to certain times and places. And this means that – no matter how exhaustive or sophisticated our approach – it will also be somewhat inaccurate.

Similarly, things like the size of a country's economy, the productivity of its businesses and the preferences of its citizens are never fixed. Indeed, even the most fundamental research in fields such as physics must account for – and attempt to mitigate against – minute constant variations, often by expending immense effort on replicating near-identical conditions between experiments.

All this leads to a vital question for almost any statistical investigation: How well does the data produced by our processes of investigation and measurement *represent* the phenomenon we are interested in – and how aware are we of the limitations of this representation?

Another way of putting this is that good statistics should be based on as *representative a sample* as possible. If, for example, you're trying to find out about the experience of running a large company, interviewing 100 random chief executives may generate some useful insights, but interviewing 100 people at random on the street probably won't. Conversely, if you're trying to find out what people consider to be the best restaurant in town, interviewing 100 people on a local street is probably better than interviewing 100 random chief executives.

Ensuring an investigation is as representative as possible is a simple-sounding principle that can be extremely complex to achieve in practice. Imagine you're interested in estimating the number of people currently infected with COVID-19 in the UK. Tracking statistics like this is vital for judging everything from the effectiveness of treatments to what measures might be taken to re-open an economy in lockdown. But how is it best done – and how far can the results be relied upon?

If the UK government were somehow able to freeze time and borrow my hypothetical drone army to conduct a 100% accurate test on every person in the country, they could determine the number of infected people precisely. Given that they can't, one of the first and most important things they can do instead is turn to the best available statistical descriptions of the UK population as a whole. That is, they can look at what they know about the overall population they're trying to assess – because you can't hope to come up with a representative sample if you don't know what you're trying to represent. In this case, the ONS has a great deal of high quality information about the UK's approximately 67 million inhabitants – so the next thing is to conduct some measurements.

Small samples generally make for less reliable results, but what's most important is how good a process you have for creating one that's as representative as possible. A few thousand people drawn from carefully selected locations are likely to yield far better insights than fifty thousand people chosen from just one town.

As I type these words (in late July 2020), approximately 160,000 coronavirus tests are being processed daily across the UK. Across the last seven days, around 0.5% of these tests have been positive. What can we infer from this? One reason it's useful to consider the percentage of tests producing a positive result – as opposed to the raw number of positives – is that this can help us compare current figures with those from the pandemic's first 'peak' in April 2020. Back then, between 10,000 and 20,000 tests were being processed daily – an order of magnitude lower than today. But as many as a third of those tests were positive on some days, a rate sixty times higher than it is now.

If we were to assume that those being tested perfectly represent the overall population this data would suggest that 0.5% of the UK's 67 million people are infected at the time of writing (335,000) versus 60% in April (40 million). But it's important to remember that even the higher figure of 160,000 daily tests remains highly *unrepresentative* when it comes to the UK population – because almost all the people being tested either have symptoms that suggest infection, or have been exposed to others who tested positive.

This is one reason that the ONS has begun additionally testing a randomized sample of the population for a so-called 'Infection Survey' that should offer more representative insights into the population as a whole, as opposed to only that subset who either have symptoms or have been exposed to the virus. The Survey's initial findings include the estimate that, during the week beginning 20 July 2020:

> 35,700 people in England had the coronavirus (95% credible interval: 23,700 to 53,200). This equates to 0.07% (95% credible interval: 0.04% to 0.10%) of the population in England or around 1 in 1,500 people (95% credible interval: 1 in 2,300 to 1 in 1,000).[36]

Over time, this study may yield vital information about national infection rates. What does it mean, though, for such a study to talk about 'credible intervals'?

Credible intervals indicate a range of values that researchers have a certain degree of confidence the actual, real-world value lies between. If a 95% credible interval suggests the number of people with coronavirus lies between 23,700 and 53,200, this implies that, if I repeated the same statistical investigation 20 times using different random samples taken from the same overall population, I would on average expect 19 out of these 20 investigations (95%) to contain the actual, real-world value within such an interval, while 1 out of 20 (5%) would not. In other words, there is a 95% chance that the actual number of infections lies within the given interval for any such investigation.

All this may sound unhelpfully complex. Why not simply say, 'the value lies between 23,700 and 53,200' or 'it's approximately 35,700?' The answer is that credible intervals are one way of expressing the workings of *probability*: that is, of communicating how statistical analyses offer not a crystal clear picture of reality, but rather a blurred series of more-or-less likely representations of it. Estimates of the number of new coronavirus infections in the UK may take the form of exact-looking totals when it comes to headlines. But these totals inexorably exist within a cloud of uncertainty that, if we wish honestly to convey what we do and don't know, it's vital to articulate. Consider the questions in Reflection Box 7.3.

Thinking About Numbers

➡ What's a future event that you feel able to predict with quite a high degree of certainty?

➡ What about one that you feel is unlikely, but still possible?

➡ What would it mean to explain your thinking clearly in each case?

Here is a final example of statistical reasoning in practice, focused on an avowedly personal question. If I am unlucky enough to become ill with COVID-19, how likely is it to kill me?

The first question this begs is simple enough: in general, what percentage of people infected with the virus go on to die of it? A figure known as the Infection Fatality Rate theoretically offers the most accurate overview here, because it bluntly states the number of people who die as a percentage of all infected individuals. In the case of COVID-19, however, both of these numbers are extremely difficult even to estimate.

As I type these words, on 6 August 2020, the World Health Organization has recorded around 702,000 deaths out of around 18,610,000 confirmed cases worldwide. This translates to around 3.8% of those confirmed to have the virus dying. But, as we've already seen, the number of confirmed cases isn't particularly representative of the number of people who have actually caught the virus, due both to the limitations of testing and the fact that the majority of people infected may not have obvious symptoms. Similarly, there's a difference between dying 'from' COVID-19 and dying 'with' COVID-19, in that a substantial number of people who tested positive may later die as a result of something else, yet still be listed among official victims. Then again, people may also die of COVID-19 but, because of the limitations of testing, not be counted among the deaths 'from' the virus.

Given all this – and the vast variations between different countries' testing, counting, health services and populations – what I need to begin answering my initial question with any accuracy is an in-depth investigation of COVID-19 deaths in the UK. Fortunately, one such study was published on 8 July 2020 in the journal *Nature*, drawing upon data from the UK's National Health Service to examine 10,926 COVID-19-related deaths over a period of three months. This study is detailed enough to help me do something important: update my highly imperfect initial estimate of the disease's risks based upon my personal situation.[37]

This principle of updating statistical beliefs in the light of new evidence is sometimes known as *Bayesian* statistics, after its 18th-century originator, Thomas Bayes. It entails a deceptively simple central observation. The likelihood that something is true, or is going to happen, can be thought of as:

- Our initial estimate of how plausible it is...
- ...modified by new evidence pertinent to the particular case we're interested in.

Most importantly, this way of thinking about statistics seeks to combine *both* prior and new knowledge into a revised view, rather than simply discarding prior knowledge in the face of new evidence.

As a male in my late 30s in good health, the *Nature* study's data suggests that my gender puts me 1.59 times more at risk than I would be if I were female; that my age puts me 16.7 times less at risk than if I were in my 50s, and a stunning 344 times less at risk than if I were aged over 80; and that my weight, habits, ethnicity and general health don't create any additional risks. In aggregate, the study suggests that – thanks almost entirely to my age – I am approximately 17 times less likely to die of COVID-19 than its 'average' victim in the UK. I can thus infer that:

- If we begin with the global figure of 3.8% case mortality (i.e. 3.8 deaths per 100 cases) as a very rough estimate for how likely any given person is to die of COVID-19 if infected...
- ...the evidence from the *Nature* study suggests we can reduce this by a factor of 17 to reflect the profile of deaths likely to 'belong' to people like me in the UK (white, male, non-smokers in good health aged under 40), giving a revised risk of around 0.2% of my dying if infected.

This is an extremely rough estimate, based on just one study and an unreliable global figure for case mortality that's almost certainly too high.

Thinking About Numbers

It doesn't factor in the potentially serious long-term health consequences of infection, any assessment of how likely I am actually to catch COVID-19, or the formal mathematics of Bayes Theorem. On a purely personal level, however, it remains reassuring.

It also highlights an important point about probability and uncertainty, which is that there is no such thing as a fixed 'chance of dying from COVID-19' out there, either for me or for anyone else. My level of risk is constantly changing, based upon factors including the current state of medical knowledge and treatments, my diet and physical condition, my mental state, my location and current activities, and so on. All that's actually out there is a constantly unfolding series of events.

Statistics can help me assess aspects of my situation in the light of what is known about other, similar situations. And things like well-designed medical studies can control these conditions effectively enough to help us learn a great deal about likely patterns and outcomes. In effect, a randomized control trial (RCT) is an exercise in creating the kind of circumstances from which it's possible to draw meaningful statistical conclusions. But while these conclusions may transform our understanding of a field or phenomenon, they remain inherently provisional and contingent: not so much prophecies as models built from measured glimpses of the world.

Through statistics, we can extend our understanding in extraordinary ways. We can sketch maps that reveal reality's patterns and possibilities – and offer guidance for reshaping both it and ourselves. But we mustn't forget what comes with this terrain: the ever-present perils of manipulation and misrepresentation; and the ongoing obligation to update our beliefs and aspirations in the light of new knowledge.[38]

Summary and recommendations

- All data is made, not found. Unless you have some awareness of the processes through which it's made, you're likely to fall into error.
- *Transparency* is one of the key properties of trustworthy statistics. By contrast, the less transparent the process of arriving at a particular statistical claim is, the more cautious you should be around it.

- Transparency on its own isn't enough, however. What's required is the meaningful contextualization of reliable information.
- The principles of 'intelligent openness' entail providing information in forms that are *Accessible, Intelligible, Assessable* and *Useable*.
- All statistics fall short of the realities you're using them to discuss. A key question is thus how well you understand the gap between reality and its statistical description.
- In particular, it's vital to account for *variability*: the fact that everything varies between different moments, places and cases.
- Statistics offer not a crystal clear reflection of reality, but rather a blur of more-or-less likely representations. Never forget that *probability* and *uncertainty* are inherent to statistical analyses.
- *A credible interval* indicates a range of values that researchers have a certain degree of confidence that the actual, real-world value lies between.
- All probabilities are *conditional* upon certain assumptions. It's vital regularly to update these assumptions.
- If our beliefs about the world don't change as we learn, something has gone wrong.

Thinking About Numbers

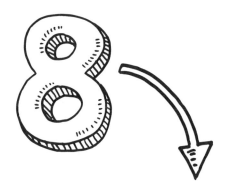

Technology and complexity: The 21st-century context

⇨ Submitting technology to scrutiny

⇨ The encoding of biases and assumptions

⇨ The myth of neutral tools

Submitting technology to scrutiny

Almost every aspect of our individual and collective lives, today, is touched upon or mediated by technology. But this doesn't make technology something easily or inherently comprehensible, whether or not we are *digital natives* (a phrase that conceals as much as it reveals). Indeed, many of the systems we use every day are specifically designed to slip beneath conscious notice: to elude understanding, manipulate perception, or present a semblance of seamless ease based upon near-incomprehensible inner workings.

This chapter is about what it means to surface these elusive, under-considered complexities: to submit technology to meaningful scrutiny and, by doing so, better equip ourselves to explore some of the 21st-century's more intractable challenges. To start things off, here is a question that invites us to dig beneath its bright surfaces: What does it mean to see the world from a machine's point of view?

One of the most important things we can do with a question like this is avoid common myths and misunderstandings – something that begins with the words we're using. No current machine can *see, consider* or *understand* the world in anything like the human sense. *Artificial Intelligence*, one of the most widely used and abused phrases in the technological lexicon, is nothing whatsoever like human intelligence; it spans entire families of algorithmic activities that have more in common with statistics than cognition. *Smart* systems aren't smart in the sense that people are; *computer memory* is nothing like *biological memory*; and, if a person is trying to think about several things at the same time, they are neither *computing, processing* nor *multitasking* in anything like the way these words were coined to describe.

Words matter: entire worldviews are at work within them. Have you ever undertaken *gig employment*, participated in the *sharing economy* or used *cloud computing*? Would you feel differently about doing these things if they were described as *insecure temporary labour, largely unregulated online asset-sweating* or *massive bunkers full of servers*?

We can make a fresh start by phrasing my question a little more precisely, and by avoiding the anthropomorphism that terms like 'seeing' and 'point of view' imply. What are some of the fundamental differences between the ways in which humans and machines deal with information?

The most obvious place to begin is with speed and volume. A computer can perform calculations billions of times faster than a person; and it can do so tirelessly and indefinitely upon trillions of bytes of data. Modern machines thrive upon ceaseless connectivity: upon oceans of information and repetitions geared towards infinity. People, meanwhile, are most dazzlingly talented when it comes to small data: to associative and imaginative leaps, to creativity and critical engagement.

Similarly, while machines trade in answers, only people can transform the world into questions and understandings – and they can only do this effectively in certain circumstances. People thrive upon serendipities, social interactions, variety and purposeful work. To treat a person like a machine is to stifle their potential: to constrict their dignity and scope. To treat a machine like a human is to indulge an all-too-human form of fantasy. Here's a list summarizing some of these distinctions:

- Information technologies process vast volumes of information at high speed.
- They thrive upon constant connectivity and repetition.
- When it comes to data and machines, bigger is almost always better.
- People, by contrast, thrive upon small amounts of meaningful information.
- The best human thinking tends to require variety, rest and purpose.
- Similarly, humans thrive upon imaginative, creative and critical engagement.
- Machines can endlessly provide answers, identify patterns and scale up processes.
- But meaningful questions and understandings only exist within human minds.

What else can we usefully add – and how might the form of my question still be misleading?

For a start, we need to dispense with any implication that humans and machines necessarily exist in some kind of competition, or that their differences automatically translate into opposition. Much of the activity in a human brain takes place beneath conscious notice;

and much of the activity that constitutes a human mind doesn't exclusively involve the brain.

Indeed, human minds aren't fully constrained or defined even by the bodies they occupy. From maps to clocks to mobile phones, countless inventions and machines contribute to our identities and augment our cognition. Meanwhile, these machines lack any direction or purpose without humans to determine their objectives. Even the most sophisticated tools are ultimately extensions of their creators' intentions: uncomprehending artefacts, relentless in their pursuit of whatever somebody has determined they should pursue.[39]

Technology, in other words, is something with which we spend our lives in constant dialogue. It's part and parcel of our societies and our identities, of our apprehensions and the connective fabric of our communities. And it's only by engaging with it as such that we can hope to view and critique our creations with any clarity. Consider the questions in Reflection Box 8.1.

REFLECTION BOX 8.1

⇨ What does the word 'technology' mean to you?

⇨ What do you consider to be the most important and useful technologies in your life?

⇨ What advice might you give to your younger self when it comes to making the most of technology?

The encoding of biases and assumptions

Here's a question I think about a lot: what follows from the permeation of our world by interconnected systems able to enact billions of decisions in the time it takes humans to make just one? Above all, I'd argue that it means humanity's collective decisions around design, data and regulation must bear the weight of vast, cascading consequences.

An automated trading system can wipe trillions of dollars off global stock markets in less than the blink of a human eye. An autonomous weapons system can execute the decision to annihilate a city with no more hesitation or remorse than a search engine expends in executing a query. A medical diagnostic system can spot early indications of cancer in 20,000 images in the time it might take a human physician to notice one. And not one of these actions means anything to the entities performing them. All of the thinking that matters – the understanding, the sense-making, the evaluation of purposes and repercussions – must either take place in human minds, or not at all.

As I type these words, it's Sunday 23 August 2020. I'm working at the weekend because the deadline for this book is looming. Around me, the consequences continue to play out of one of the pandemic's more unexpected scandals: one centred on algorithms.

Specifically, the scandal concerns the British government's approval of an algorithm to generate exam results for the nation's schoolchildren: an unprecedented response to an unprecedented situation. It's necessary because, with every school in the country closed because of the pandemic, no schoolchildren have been able to sit any exams – but exam results are considered vital both for assessment and for determining entry into further education or employment. The process used to generate substitute results went something like this:

i As occurs in a normal school year, teachers supplied a predicted grade for each pupil in each exam, with these exam predictions providing the basis for applications to universities, jobs, and so on.

ii Additionally, teachers were asked to rank all pupils taking a particular exam in order of likely achievement, resulting in a complete rank order of students for each subject at each school, from the most to the least able.

iii Rather than use the predicted grades to generate results, the ranking data was put through an algorithm which factored in the past three years of overall performance in each subject at each school, then used this data to allocate a grade to each student based upon their rank and the historical range of results for their subject at their school. This was intended to avoid so-called 'grade inflation', where over-generous predictions might otherwise produce more high grades than in previous years.

iv In order to avoid producing unreliable results on the basis of inadequate data, the algorithm was also designed to attach less weight to the last three years of results if a subject was only taken by between five and fifteen entrants at a school. If fewer than five students at a school were entered for a subject, the only factor determining grades was the teacher's prediction.

What did this system look like in practice? If, say, a school had seen only one 'A' grade per year for Maths in each of the last three years, the algorithm would stop teachers awarding a dozen 'A' grades this year. Even if such a school's maths teacher were to predict a dozen 'A' grades, almost all of these grades would be lowered in order to bring results in line with previous years – a process backed up by overarching statistical efforts to ensure that no particular region, ethnic group or gender ended up worse off (on average) than in previous years.

In other words, the results were engineered to be 'fair' in terms of past years and overall distribution. In order to achieve this, students' results were essentially treated as the products of their school rather than of individual efforts. What do you make of such a system and its likely effects? Consider the questions in Reflection Box 8.2.

///REFLECTION BOX 8.2

⇨ Can you think of any potential problems with the system I've outlined above?

⇨ What kind of schools and students might it benefit?

⇨ Under what circumstances might someone feel that the algorithm had treated them unfairly?

//

Here's what happened next. On 13 August 2020, the results of the above system were announced for the A-level exams taken by school-leavers in England, Wales and Northern Ireland. Almost 40% of the

Technology and Complexity

final results produced by the algorithm were lower than teachers' assessments. Given that students knew what their predicted grades were – and many had offers to attend university courses contingent on achieving these predictions – the result was an outpouring of discontent, with some teenagers even taking to the streets in anti-algorithmic demonstrations.

This disappointment was understandable, not least because being allocated a grade without having a chance to prove your ability is self-evidently less satisfactory than giving an exam your best shot. But was the system genuinely unfair?

One way of answering this is to consider what the algorithm meant if you were a teenager attending a below-average school – the kind of school more likely to be found in a deprived area – which, in the previous three years, had never seen anyone achieve better than a grade 'C' at maths A-Level. This year, perhaps, the school has been performing better under an ambitious new head teacher; and you are, perhaps, a talented mathematician who has received an offer to study maths at a leading university, so long as you achieve an 'A' grade. You have studied hard. Your teacher has confidently predicted you an 'A' and ranked you as the most able student in your year. Yet none of this matters, because a 'C' is the best possible grade the historic data suggests a student at your school can achieve in maths – and a 'C' is thus almost certainly what the algorithm will award you.

So far as this particular algorithm is concerned, history and circumstances are destiny. There is little possibility of someone in disadvantaged circumstances out-performing their school's track record. If your school has historically had several students each year get a bottom 'U' grade in maths, being ranked among the bottom few students will almost certainly get you a 'U' too – even if your prediction is a 'D' or 'C'.

If, however, you attend a school with a history of high achievement, the range of possible results your grade is drawn from will be matchingly high. Perhaps the top ten maths students will all automatically get 'A' grades, while even the lowest may still get a 'C'. Or if you are either studying a subject few people are taking or attend a small school – both conditions more likely to apply to expensive private schools than to large state-funded schools – your teacher's prediction are more likely to help your grade.

In aggregate, you could argue that this was a fair system, in that it produced overall results in line with previous years and trends. As I explored in the third chapter, however, what 'fairness' means is open to passionate dispute; and this particular version of fairness fell foul of several strongly held assumptions.

In the end, it took less than a week for the government to announce that the results provided by the algorithm would be discarded and teachers' unmodified predictions used instead. This was a political rather than a statistical decision, but it pointed to a recognition that the desire algorithmically to safeguard academic standards had trampled upon the intuition that exam grades should be connected to individual potential and performance.

Interestingly, it wasn't the fact that 40% of students had failed to make their predicted grades that proved fatal (this figure isn't that dissimilar to the difference between predictions and results in a 'normal' year). Rather, it was the fact that this particular algorithmic assessment manifestly and implacably entrenched existing inequalities, while leaving little scope for appeal, correction or debate.

By minimizing any variability above and beyond a school's recent history, the connection between effort and achievement that exams inherently seek to reward was broken. The privileged were disproportionately rewarded *en masse*, the less privileged disproportionately penalized, and exceptional individual efforts ignored. As the author and broadcaster Timandra Harkness put it in an 18 August article, the prospect of being judged by such an algorithm was:

> closer to buying car insurance than taking an exam for which
> you have worked for nearly two years. Just enter postcode, make
> and model and we will predict your likelihood of making a claim,
> and hence your premium.[40]

What I've offered is a simplified account of a statistical model, as all such accounts tend to be. But it highlights something the mathematician Hannah Fry anatomizes in her 2018 book *Hello World: How to be Human in the Age of the Machine*, which is that the fair and successful deployment of a technology relies upon an ethically and critically engaged account of the problems that technology is trying to solve – and a careful awareness of its inputs' limitations. 'Using algorithms as a mirror to reflect the real world isn't always helpful,' she notes, 'especially when the mirror is reflecting a present reality that only exists because of centuries of bias'.[41]

In the case of the exam results algorithm itself, Fry offered a handy checklist (via Twitter) of the ways in which its deployment fell short:

- Impossible problem expecting a magical solution.
- Over-complicated solution.
- In-built bias.
- Over-trust in equations.
- Total lack of transparency.
- No easy way to appeal.

What do you make of these six points? As you may have noticed, the majority of them don't actually refer to the algorithm at all. Instead, they describe the human attitudes, expectations and structures of transparency and appeal surrounding it. That is, they're about the mistaken belief that a wickedly complex question (*'what grades would the UK's schoolchildren have received if they had been able to take exams as normal in 2020?'*) could adequately be resolved by getting a machine to solve a far simpler question (*'given a rank ordering of students in each school, what would it mean to assign them grades that preserved the same pattern of exam results schools saw over the last three years?'*) – and that this solution required only a minimal level of accountability and explanation.

This is a problem far from unique to examination results. Indeed, one of the most striking things about this case study is not so much its egregiousness as the fact that its egregiousness made headlines and forced a government U-turn.

In the normal order of things, automated over-simplifications and injustices tend to be noted and lamented only by small numbers of people, if at all. Thousands of CVs are automatically sorted and selected every day on the basis of proxies for race, gender and class rather than ability. Search engines reiterate biases around everything from race and gender to careers and criminality, as do machine learning systems. To search online for images associated with high-status careers has, historically, been to summon photographs of middle-aged white men.

Similarly, credit rating and loan approval systems aggregate data that may condemn those from certain backgrounds, or resident in certain areas, to vastly higher costs than otherwise identical applicants; while libraries of text and images used for training AI systems can impart hosts of prejudices, ranging from the gendering of jobs to the desirability of different body types.[42]

For a scandal to break through to the realm of mainstream outrage required, among other things, it to feature among the experiences of those unaccustomed to suffering structural injustice.

The myth of neutral tools

None of the above means that technology is 'bad' any more than its life-enhancing applications make it 'good'. What it emphasizes, rather, is the absurdity of evaluating any technology in isolation from the circumstances of its development, design and deployment; and of the dangers that accompany seeing the world as a series of problems awaiting technological solutions. How can we do better? Consider the questions in Reflection Box 8.3.

REFLECTION BOX 8.3

⇨ What does it mean, to you, to use technology well?

⇨ Which technologies do you most admire and enjoy?

⇨ Which are you most worried about? Why?

Despite the critique I've set out above, the technologies of our information age are both non-optional and a tremendous gift – the greatest and farthest-reaching engines of research, investigation, explanation and intellectual enhancement in history. Used wisely, computation offers wholly new forms of power, collaboration and understanding; insights into complexities inconceivable even a few decades ago; analyses of intractable problems and challenges that can liberate and empower us as never before.

What's holding us back, as I hope this brief discussion has emphasized, is not so much the nature of our tools as the blinkered and wishful assumptions we foist upon them: the unaccountable injustices, category errors and encoded biases lurking behind the rhetoric of machine impartiality and efficiency. And that's before you get to the deployment of ever-more-powerful technologies for exploitation, profit, authoritarian law enforcement, the destruction of privacy, and much else besides – often behind the rubric of innovation, security and efficiency.

When it comes to technological myths, perhaps the most pernicious of all is embodied in the plea that 'tools are neutral – it's how we use them that matters'. It's a deceptively appealing call for common sense and personal responsibility. Yet, I would argue, if there's just one lesson we should take to heart when it comes to technology, it's this: there is no such thing as a neutral system or tool.

To pick up a gun is to walk through a world populated by potential targets: to extend your agency in the direction of a brutal and particular violence. To step into a car is to transform the significance of distances and landscapes; to become part of a vast apparatus of convenience, regulation and profit. To select the data and criteria upon which an algorithm will operate is to choose what counts, and how much. To determine the mechanisms of transparency, explicability and appeal around such an algorithm is to assert a series of fundamental beliefs around what constitutes fairness and accountability, and what is (or isn't) owed to those whose lives it affects.

Technological neutrality is, at best, a misleading fiction, and at worst a cynical evasion of scrutiny and responsibility. Precisely because of the complexity of the systems we are creating and enmeshed in, the question of what we want *from* technology matters more than ever: of what values, assumptions and regulations are desirable when it comes to automated systems' embodiment of society's fundamental contracts and relationships. As John D. Sterman, director of the MIT Systems Dynamics Group, put it in a 2011 article exploring so-called 'side-effects' in the context of complex systems:

> There are no side effects – just effects. Those we expected or that prove beneficial we call the main effects and claim credit. Those that undercut our policies and cause harm we claim to be side effects, hoping to excuse the failure of our intervention. 'Side effects' are not a feature of reality but a sign that the boundaries of our mental models are too narrow, our time horizons too short.[43]

We must, in other words, attempt to assess complex systems and challenges – which include, but are far from restricted to, the technological domain – not according to special or selective pleadings, but rather in the context of all their impacts. If social media are affecting electoral politics, we cannot simply wall off the digital realm from the 'real world' as if these were distinct domains, or 'online behaviour' a category of action separate from all others. If automated surveillance is eroding privacy and legal norms, we must ask what kind of a society we wish to live in – and how far certain business models and political priorities are or aren't compatible with basic freedoms.

In the end, there is no algorithmic solution coming to save us: no one perspective to be optimized towards, no machine superintelligence waiting to dissolve humanity's collective dilemmas. There is only the ongoing, plural negotiation of knowing ourselves a little better; of testing and improving our knowledge, alongside the systems that sustain it; and of honestly attempting to trace the chains of intended and unintended consequences which girdle our world.

Summary and recommendations

- The words we use matter, especially when it comes to technology. From *AI* to the *gig economy*, from *cloud computing* to *memory* and *processing*, the assumptions and analogies embedded in language can end up doing our thinking for us.
- It's not meaningful or useful to treat technology as distinct from the circumstances of its design and use. Technology is part and parcel of our societies and our identities, our knowledge and the connective fabric of our communities.
- The speed and scale of technology's impacts are a defining feature of the challenge they pose to human understanding.
- Collective decisions around *design*, *data* and *regulation* bear vast, cascading consequences, and need meaningfully to be debated in advance (and scrutinized during deployment) if they are to be controlled.
- The fair and successful deployment of a technology depends upon an ethically and critically engaged account of the problems it is trying to solve – and a careful awareness of its inputs' limitations.

- One of the most pervasive and pernicious myths about technology is that tools are neutral, and it's how we use them that really matters.
- Instead, try to assess the particular *affordances* of systems and technologies: the behaviours and attitudes they facilitate and inhibit; the perspectives they align with; the people they benefit; the consequences of using them, or of refusing.
- Precisely because of the complexity of the systems we are creating and enmeshed in, the question of what we want *from* technology matters more than ever.
- There are *no side-effects* – just effects. Assess complex systems and challenges in the light of lived experience, without boxing off undesirable or unintended consequences from whatever is claimed to be their purpose.

And finally...

As I type these words, it's Wednesday 26 August 2020. I am seated at my desk, at home, looking back over the first few sentences of this book. I wrote those sentences five months ago, and there's a phrase within them that already looks woefully naïve: 'in the middle of the COVID-19 pandemic'.

This is how I described my situation on 26 March 2020, two weeks after the World Health Organization first characterized COVD-19 as a pandemic. Since then, approximately 23.3 million cases of coronavirus and 795,000 deaths have been officially confirmed worldwide. It's still too soon to know where we are in the course of things – and this will probably continue to be true until, one way or another, treatments and vaccinations restore some version of life as it used to be. Cases are currently low in my home country, the UK; but they're high or rising in plenty of other places, with the long uncertainties of the northern hemisphere's winter yet to come.

Was my turn of phrase accidental, or did I genuinely hope that March might mark the 'middle' of what was unfolding? I can't remember. It would be easy, now, for me to substitute the phrase 'at the beginning of the COVID-19 pandemic' or remove the reference entirely. But I'm glad my ignorance has been preserved. As I've tried to emphasize during the course of this book, retrospect is seductive when it comes to both thinking and writing. Few things are more comforting than claiming you knew in advance which way the story would end – and few tricks are easier to pull off when you're the one writing the story.

To think is, in part, to turn the world into stories: to weave coherence out of events. I've spent much of this book exploring what it means to attempt this without, so far as possible, betraying the world's complexities and uncertainties. But both complexity and uncertainty will always be greater than our capacity to constrain them – and so the mismatch will always be there too, inviting us to assume and presume, to cling onto saving beliefs rather than face the scale of our ignorance.

If this sounds gloomy, it isn't meant to be. Writing this book has been, for me, one of the great satisfactions of this strange and anxious year; a chance to speak with as much honesty and clarity as I can muster about things I believe in. To become less deceived; to change our opinions when the facts change; to open our minds to others' views while keeping our critical faculties sharp: all of these can make our world a little more hopeful. And, as the pandemic and its attendant conspiracies have all too vividly illustrated, the alternative is not a strategy that ends well for our species (although plenty of people may profit from it in the meantime).

What, if anything, have you found useful or memorable during the course of this book? In the final Reflection Box, for the last time, there are some questions for you to consider.

FINAL REFLECTION BOX

⇨ What would you say is the most important or interesting thing you've read in this book?

⇨ Why? How might you explain it to someone else?

⇨ What have you read that you've disagreed with?

⇨ What has surprised you, or made you think twice?

⇨ Is there anything you felt was missing?

If you want to share your responses to these questions with me (or any other queries and comments), I'm on Twitter at @TomChatfield. Or you can drop me a line via my website at tomchatfield.net. I can't promise a reply, but I'll try my best.

In the end, perhaps the most important thing all of us can do is keep talking to one another – and trying truly to listen to what is being said in response. As I emphasized in my chapter on clarity and language, almost all worthwhile writing is bound up with reading and re-writing; and almost all worthwhile thinking with reflection and re-thinking. Words are slippery, remarkable, exquisite things. And perhaps the most remarkable fact of all is that they can, like many of our creations, sometimes become better and wiser than the people they begin with – and help them to become better in turn.

This is one more thing that effective writing and thinking have in common: the fact that it's apparatuses of habit, research, iteration, collaboration and communication that allow us to bring forth further-reaching results than anything we might accomplish unaided. All of us are the products of our times, our environments and our relationships – and it's through more closely scrutinizing the dialogue between these contexts and our own natures that many of life's most important insights can be found.

What should you take away from this book? I hope you'll have gained a degree of pleasure from it. But there are also some points that I consider important enough to spell out one last time (you are, as ever, more than welcome to disagree):

- There are few things that any of us have enough knowledge and experience of to be able to deal with entirely unassisted.
- In order to start learning, you need to think as clearly as possible about the gaps in your knowledge, experience and expertise – and how to redress these.
- When our knowledge is uncertain or provisional, the evolving nature of this uncertainty itself becomes the truth it is our duty to communicate.
- Cultivate the language of reasoned uncertainty in yourself. Beware of certainty in the absence of evidence among others.
- No matter how clearly something is expressed, it also needs to be read closely for it to succeed as an act of communication.

- Try to engage with others' ideas attentively and carefully, taking the time to consider and spell out their assumptions. Finding your own words for their key ideas is often the best way to clarify what's going on.
- It's vastly more comfortable to assume that our emotional intuitions can be translated into hard-and-fast rules about the world than it is to assume that they are, at best, useful in some circumstances. Unfortunately, this latter situation is the one we actually live in.
- To constructively challenge an assumption, you need to reinstate difficult questions in the place of over-simplifications; and to find not only an intellectual common ground with others, but also common values and purposes.
- Spelling out the reasoning behind something allows you to see why someone believes it, assess how convincing you find this reasoning, compare it to other lines of reasoning – and then to make an informed decision about whether to accept it.
- Always consider a variety of lines of reasoning when analysing something important. So far as possible, try to restate someone else's thinking in a way they agree is fair, then to explain where you do and don't agree with them – and why.
- It is possible endlessly to confirm anything you wish to believe if all you do is look for examples that support it. By contrast, attempting to falsify an explanation allows you to test it against rival explanations, and to explore which is better.
- Wherever possible, seek falsification over confirmation; and don't be seduced by a theory that it's impossible to disprove. To explain everything is to explain nothing.
- Creativity isn't a luxury or an innate talent. It's a process that anyone can engage in, if they practice the right method – and that can benefit everyone.
- Remember that nobody controls the reception of their work. The only guarantee is that you need to begin, and then to keep going, in order to create something.
- If you want to know what's going on, dig into the stories behind a statistical claim. Try to understand the gap between reality and its statistical description.

And Finally...

- Machines trade in answers, and offer power and scope vastly beyond the human; but only people can transform the world into questions.
- In the end, all the thinking that matters – the understanding, the evaluation of purposes and repercussions – must either take place in human minds, or not at all.

Thank you for reading, for thinking, and (I hope) for having at least a few second thoughts.

A toolkit for clearer thinking: Ten key concepts

⇨ Arguments   ⇨ Doubt

⇨ Assumptions   ⇨ Explanations

⇨ Attention   ⇨ Fallacies

⇨ Charity   ⇨ Rhetoric

⇨ Confirmation   ⇨ Variability

One: Arguments

In a philosophical argument (as opposed to a shouting match), a final *conclusion* is justified by a *premise* or linked series of premises. Spelling out and analysing these premises in *standard form* can help us to see *why* someone believes something is the case; to identify any implicit or faulty *assumptions*; and to compare different lines of reasoning. By contrast, an *assertion* simply states something is the case, without offering any reasoning in support.

A *deductive* argument uses logic to derive a conclusion from its premises. If its reasoning is *valid* and its premises are true, its conclusion must also be true: this is called a *sound argument*. By contrast, an *inductive* argument invokes patterns and observations to suggest that a conclusion is *likely* to be true. We can express any inductive argument in deductive form by making explicit the assumption that the balance of probabilities supports it. This doesn't create any additional certainty, but can *clarify* things.

In general, carefully spelling out your and others' reasoning is an excellent way of ensuring you think about an issue as rigorously as possible. But don't forget to do so *charitably* rather than just building *straw men* (see below).

Two: Assumptions

Anything we take for granted but don't make explicit is an assumption. We can never make all our assumptions explicit, or get to the bottom of them: you always have to begin somewhere. But you can try to examine and debate *relevant assumptions* in the context of reasoning.

Many of our deepest assumptions are emotional and instinctual, drawing upon our biological and cultural heritage. To critique these can feel like an assault. But even these can be discussed and, under some circumstances, reconciled or adapted. In particular, having a *common purpose* can help a group turn a diversity of assumptions into a benefit, provided these are discussed with *mutual respect*.

Given that respectful debate is by no means guaranteed, an *intolerance of intolerance* is itself an important principle: that is, insisting that violent intolerance of the peaceful exchange of views is itself intolerable.

Three: Attention

Managing your time and attention is a particularly significant challenge in our digital age, when both immeasurable informational riches and distractions can crowd into every moment. In this context, there can be a tremendous liberating power in giving yourself permission to *pause* and think twice – and in knowing when a pause is, and isn't, worthwhile.

People require different types and textures of time in their lives to think and to live well: boundaries, divisions; rest, recuperation and time for the mind to wander. Consciously exploring your own habits and preferences is a vital way of working out what it means to find a way of *working that works for you*. Don't let all your time turn into the same kind of time.

Four: Charity

In philosophy, the *principle of charity* describes our duty to extract the maximum possible reasonable content from what other people say and do – and to refrain from assuming malice or error on their part unless we have compelling reasons to think otherwise.

This isn't about being nice for its own sake (although it does presume the value of civil disagreement). Rather, it's a way of ensuring you learn as much as possible from views different from your own; that you submit your own beliefs to the best possible test; and that you engage empathetically and rigorously with those who disagree with you. You should also be prepared to change your own mind in the face of compelling new evidence.

All of this can prove extremely difficult in practice – and may not apply to disagreements conducted in bad faith, or where violence or intolerance are integral to someone else's perspective. As a guiding principle, charitable engagement with others' ideas is a valuable form of emotional and intellectual self-discipline. If in doubt, don't assume yourself to be right or righteous. Ask open questions of others, and listen carefully to their responses. You may be surprised by what they say.

Five: Confirmation

Confirmation bias describes people's tendency to primarily seek out (and attend to) only information that confirms whatever they already believe, or might wish to be true. Confirmation bias is to a degree inevitable, in the sense that all of us experience the world through the prism of our own perceptions, and draw most readily in our day-to-day thinking upon that which feels most familiar or significant.

Confirmation bias, like other cognitive biases, tends to be at its most pernicious when we are bombarded with information we're ill-equipped to assess unaided, or when we are exposed to deliberate behavioural manipulations or *disinformation*. It's thus vital when facing difficult questions to *slow down* and to *seek cognitive reinforcements* in the form of others' views, reliable external information, or an informative reframing of the issue at hand.

Six: Doubt

To doubt something *constructively* is to suspend judgement and, rather than leaping towards the comforts of certainty, to instead take an active interest in identifying what you do not know – and what it might mean reliably to redress this ignorance. Psychologically, doubt can be difficult to sustain, even taboo; especially in contexts that place a premium upon the rapid expression of attention-grabbing certainties, such as social media.

How can we deal with the difficulty of expressing doubt – and of ensuring it is heard and heeded? This is partly a structural question, relating to the incentives embedded in information systems and the dynamics of public debate. But it's also important to remember that honest doubt is ultimately better able to describe and predict reality than wishful certainties and denials; and that it can, by allowing us to explore different types of uncertainty, help make a case for decisive early actions in the face of catastrophic or exponential risks.

Seven: Explanations

To explain something is to offer good reasons for *why* things are the way they are. In general, the best explanations manage to account for everything we know while being as simple as possible. By contrast, inadequate explanations either deny inconvenient evidence or tie themselves up in needless complexity.

There is no rule that explanations *must* be simple – which makes it important to *compare* different explanations in terms of their usefulness and precision at describing and predicting reality. A *conspiracy theory* is an explanation that, by seeking to explain everything within its circular and confirmatory logic, ends up explaining nothing.

In general, any explanation that is immune to disproof is worth little. By contrast, an explanation that yields testable predictions is one that can improve our knowledge and understanding whether or not these predictions come true (because we can either adopt it as a working model, or treat it as usefully falsified). The ultimate prize of such investigations is a detailed, predictive *theory* that has passed the most rigorous tests we can muster – and which thus offers a powerful basis for understanding the world.

Eight: Fallacies

A *fallacy* is a form of faulty or flawed reasoning – and, in particular, one that may at first glance appear compelling. In general, fallacies smuggle faulty hidden assumptions into lines of argument or justification, and are best dealt with by making these assumptions *explicit*.

One common fallacy is an *ad hominem* argument, which suggests that a point of view can be dismissed purely because of who expressed it, as opposed to its content. We can skewer such a fallacy by noting that, for example, the truth of a statement such as 'two plus two is four' isn't affected by who is saying it. Another common fallacy is a *false dichotomy*, which wrongly implies that a complex question can be reduced to two mutually exclusive options – and thus that, if one doesn't apply, the other must.

It remains important to be *charitable* in the philosophical sense when analysing fallacies, and to realize that they may entail not so much a wholly incorrect claim as a *faulty generalization*. An *appeal to nature*, for example, may wrongly seek to resolve a complex question by implying that 'anything that is unnatural must be bad'. But this doesn't mean that associating 'natural' things with good outcomes is entirely without merit. It may simply mean that the merits of such a view have been exaggerated, misunderstood or miscategorized.

Nine: Rhetoric

While a fallacy is by definition a faulty form of reasoning, *rhetoric* describes the persuasive use of language in the broadest sense. It's thus something that it is important to be sensitive towards, but that isn't 'bad' any more than it is 'good'. In particular, it's important to note that *all language has some rhetorical qualities*, and that a purportedly neutral or impartial tone can have as much rhetorical impact as a highly emotional one.

When engaging with rhetoric, it's useful to distinguish between the emotive effects of someone's tone and language versus the informational content of their words. As in the case of fallacies, explicitly spelling out the rhetorical impact of a particular piece of communication can go a long way towards clarifying your thinking – as can being aware of the rhetorical components of your own work.

Ten: Variability

Given how tricky it can be to think clearly about statistics, one of the simplest and most important points to remember is that all statistics are *made* rather than found – and that there will thus always be a *gap* between the statistics you are looking at and the actual thing you are interested in.

In particular, *variability* describes the fact that most phenomena we investigate via statistics vary between different times and places, and that our thinking must take this variability into account. Assessing the population of a country, for example, entails making certain measurements and assessments, then extrapolating from these to an overall estimate. This may be accurate and reliable to an impressive degree – but it's important to remember that the country's *actual* population is a number that is never fixed for more than a few moments, and can only ever be imperfectly known.

We can learn an immense amount about our world through statistics, but this learning will be at its most rigorous if we remember that *the processes through which statistical knowledge is manufactured* should themselves be as much our subject as the phenomena they describe.

Endnotes and further readings

How to use this book

1 Robert Poynton, *Do/Pause: You are Not a To Do List* (The Do Book Co., 2019). You can read the first chapter for free online at https://medium.com/do-book-company/you-are-not-a-to-do-list-42ab27994e72 and find Poynton's 7 April 2020 lecture, 'Why we all need to pause right now', at www.youtube.com/watch?v=vhefsrZ87g8.

Introduction

2 This has become one of Kierkegaard's most famous lines, and comes from a passage in his 1843 journal which, in literal translation, reads: 'It is really true what philosophy tells us, that life must be understood backwards. But with this, one forgets the second proposition, that it must be lived forwards. A proposition which, the more it is subjected to careful thought, the more it ends up concluding precisely that life at any given

moment cannot really ever be fully understood; exactly because there is no single moment where time stops completely in order for me to take position [to do this]: going backwards' (Søren Kierkegaard, Journalen JJ: 167 (1843), Søren Kierkegaards Skrifter, Søren Kierkegaard Research Center, Copenhagen, 1997–, vol. 18, p. 306).

3 In February 2020, Victor Adebowale edited a special edition of the *British Medical Journal* exploring racism in medicine, which includes wide-ranging reflections on systematic racial inequalities in health and healthcare: see vol. 368, issue 8233, 15 February 2020. As Adebowale put it in a 28 October 2020 interview with the BMJ, reflecting upon the pandemic and societal inequalities in the UK, 'in some ways, what covid has done is exploit the weaknesses in society … It has poured red paint down all the cracks. You can see the inequality, the inequity, the need for innovation. It has just made it so stark that we have to deal with these things' (BMJ 2020; 371: m4111).

4 One common example of availability bias is the way recent or memorable events tend to dominate public attitudes: when someone famous is publicly struggling with a rare cancer, for example, which subsequently attracts high levels of attention and funding. The related phenomenon of *cognitive dissonance* – where decisions made in the face of conflicting evidence are justified on the basis of personal beliefs – is accessibly explored by social psychologists Carol Tavris and Elliot Aronson in *Mistakes Were Made (but Not by Me)* (Pinter & Martin, 2020).

5 Annette Simmons, *The Story Factor* (Basic Books, 2019), p. 33. As Simmons notes in her first chapter, the power of stories harnesses phenomena like availability bias, inviting people to take possession of ideas that might otherwise seem irrelevant: 'Telling a meaningful story means inspiring your listeners … to reach the same conclusions you have reached and decide *for themselves* to believe what you say and do what you want them to do. People value their own conclusions more highly than yours.

They will only have faith in a story that has become real for them personally' (Ibid, p. 3).

1 Attention and reflection

6 John Dewey, *How We Think* (DC Heath & Co., 1910), p. 13. You can find the entire text online via Project Gutenberg at www.gutenberg.org/files/37423/37423-h/37423-h.htm, or read it in book form in the 2003 edition from Dover Publications. For a contrasting perspective, drawing upon and extending many of Dewey's insights, *Critical Thinking* (Routledge, 2010) by bell hooks offers a powerful vision for progressive, critically engaged education in the present day.

7 When it comes to Aristotle and habit, the philosopher Edith Hall's *Aristotle's Way* (Penguin, 2019) makes a careful case for the contemporary uses of his philosophy. 'The only way to be a good person is to do good things', Hall argues, after Aristotle. 'You have to treat people with fairness repeatedly.' (p. 9)

8 For the *Nature* letter, see Andersen, K.G., Rambaut, A., Lipkin, W.I., et al. (2020) 'The proximal origin of SARS-CoV-2', Nat Med 26, 450–452, https://doi.org/10.1038/s41591-020-0820-9, published 17 March 2020. For Donald Trump's comment on the WHO, see 'Coronavirus: Trump stands by China lab origin theory for virus', BBC News, 1 May 2020, www.bbc.co.uk/news/world-us-canada-52496098. For a thorough account of the Wuhan Institute of Virology origin debate, see Eliza Barclay, 'Why these scientists still doubt the coronavirus leaked from a Chinese lab', *Vox*, 29 April 2020, www.vox.com/2020/4/23/21226484/wuhan-lab-coronavirus-china.

9 The affect heuristic describes rapid emotional responses that allow us to make fast, intuitive judgement. For a profound investigation of the interweaving of emotion with identity and rationality, see the philosopher Martha Nussbaum's *Upheavals of Thought: The Intelligence of Emotions* (Cambridge, 2003). 'Emotions', she argues, 'are not just the fuel that powers the psychological mechanism of a reasoning creature, they are parts, highly complex and messy parts, of this creature's reasoning itself' (p. 3).

10 In *The Prospect Interview* #127: 'Behind the science of Covid-19', 28 April 2020, online at https://play.acast.com/s/headspace2/-127-howbesttohandlecovid-19-withadamkucharski.

2 Working with words

11 James Gleick tells this story in his biography *Genius: The Life and Science of Richard Feynman* (Pantheon, 1992), p. 399: 'In 1964 [Feynman] had made the rare decision to serve on a public commission, responsible for choosing mathematics textbooks for California's grade schools … He argued to his fellow commissioners that sets [i.e. set theory], as presented in the reformers' textbooks, were an example of the most insidious pedantry: new definitions for the sake of definition, a perfect case of introducing words without introducing ideas … In the real world, he pointed out … absolute precision is an ideal that can never be reached.' For a taste of Feynman's own lucid explanations of complex ideas, *The Feynman Lectures on Physics* are available online in full at www.feynmanlectures.caltech.edu.

12 John Searle, *Intentionality: An Essay in the Philosophy of Mind* (Cambridge, 1983), p. x. For a rich alternative view on the nature of minds and language, see Ruth Garrett Millika, *Varieties of Meaning: The 2002 Jean Nicod Lectures* (MIT Press, 2006).

13 For an inspiring embodiment of rhetoric as a force for good, *The Meaning of Freedom* (City Lights, 2012) by the author and activist Angela Davis collects a series of eloquent, impassioned speeches advocating change and resistance to injustice. 'Wherever I am, whatever I happen to be doing', she writes, 'I try to feel connected to futures that are only possible through struggle' (p. 36).

14 Sherry Turkle, *Reclaiming Conversation: The Power of Talk in a Digital Age* (Penguin, 2015) p. 62. In the digital context, Turkle's exploration of life online *Alone Together: Why We Expect More from Technology and Less from Each Other* (Basic Books, 2017) is also excellent.

3 The importance of assumptions

15 The US Centers for Disease Control and Prevention website has a useful potted history of smallpox at www.cdc.gov/smallpox/history/history.html.

16 When it comes to societies' deepest divisions, among the most powerful words I've read are those of author and activist Audre Lorde in her 1981 speech 'The Uses of Anger: Women Responding to Racism', which speaks both of her anger in the face of racism and the ways in which others have striven to dismiss it: 'I speak out of direct and particular anger at an academic conference, and a white woman says, "Tell me how you feel but don't say it too harshly or I cannot hear you." But is it my manner that keeps her from hearing, or the threat of a message that her life may change?' The full text is available online at www.blackpast.org/african-american-history/speeches-african-american-history/1981-audre-lorde-uses-anger-women-responding-racism.

17 Hume's line on reason being 'the slave of the passions' can be found in Book Two, Part Three, Section Three of *A Treatise of Human Nature*, online in full at www.gutenberg.org/ebooks/4705.

18 Jonathan Haidt, *The Righteous Mind: Why Good People Are Divided by Politics and Religion* (Penguin, 2013), p. 90. For an illuminating perspective on a different kind of unexamined assumption, Rebecca Solnit's 2008 essay 'Men Explain Things to Me' can be read online at www.guernicamag.com/rebecca-solnit-men-explain-things-to-me or in her 2014 essay collection of the same name. At its heart is the story of a man so accustomed to assuming the role of authoritative explainer that he explains *one of Solnit's own books* to her at length, without letting her get in enough words to tell him that she in fact wrote it.

19 Marianne Williamson, *The Healing of America* (Simon & Schuster, 1997), p. 72; a book that makes a powerful ethical and spiritual case for political renewal.

20 Daniel Kahneman, *Thinking, Fast and Slow* (Farrar, Strauss and Giroux, 2011), p. 12; a bestselling book that remains a lucid, essential introduction to the principles underpinning much current research into cognitive bias and heuristics.

4 Giving good reasons

21 The *Washington Post* reproduced a full transcript of the Meet the Press interview in which 'alternative facts' were born on 22 January 2017, under the headline 'How Kellyanne Conway ushered in the era of alternative facts' – see www.washingtonpost.com/news/the-fix/wp/2017/01/22/how-kellyanne-conway-ushered-in-the-era-of-alternative-facts. Conway's subsequent interview with Mark Simone of New York's 710 WOR Radio was discussed in *Salon* on 1 February 2018 under the headline 'Kellyanne Conway: The American people "have their own facts"' – see www.salon.com/2018/02/01/kellyanne-conway-the-american-people-have-their-own-set-of-facts.

22 Walter Sinnott-Armstrong's book *Think Again: How to Reason and Argue* (Pelican, 2018) is a lucid account of the everyday power and significance of reasoning, including a broad take on arguments that encompasses their uses and abuses.

23 For an interactive complement to this chapter's topics, the free online course 'Logical and Critical Thinking' offered by the University of Auckland's FutureLearn project at www.futurelearn.com/courses/logical-and-critical-thinking contains stimulating exercises, examples and videos explaining concepts in detail.

24 If you want to explore the moral significance of reasoning, Mary Midgley's wise and accessible book *What Is Philosophy for?* (Bloomsbury, 2018) is a fine place to start.

5 Seeking good explanations

25 In his 26 November 2012 article for *The Conversation*, 'Straw man science: keeping climate simple' – online at https://theconversation.com/straw-man-science-keeping-climate-simple-10782 – Michael J.I. Brown offers a model (and horribly prophetic) takedown of straw man arguments against climate change at the time.

26 In a 28 April 2020 report for the Harvard Kennedy School's *Misinformation Review*, 'Why do people believe COVID-19 conspiracy theories?' – online at https://misinforeview.

hks.harvard.edu/article/why-do-people-believe-covid-19-conspiracy-theories – nine scholars surveyed 2,023 US adults and analysed their beliefs about COVID-19. They found that '29% of respondents agree that the threat of COVID-19 has been exaggerated to damage President Trump; 31% agree that the virus was purposefully created and spread' – and that 'the strongest predictors of beliefs in these ideas are a psychological predisposition to reject expert information and accounts of major events (denialism), a psychological predisposition to view major events as the product of conspiracy theories (conspiracy thinking), and partisan and ideological motivations'.

27 Confirmation bias is much-discussed in the context of 'filter bubbles', which describe the tendency of online platforms to present people with news and views similar to their own, thus confirming rather than challenging existing beliefs. If you want to burst your filter bubble, seek out multiple perspectives on newsworthy topics (and multiple takes on what's newsworthy in the first place); aim to follow interesting people from a wide variety of backgrounds on social media, newsletters and podcasts; and use search engines like duckduckgo to see results that aren't tailored to your profile or history.

28 Karl Popper, *The Logic of Scientific Discovery* (Routledge, 2002), p. 431. Perhaps the best accessible introduction to Popper's thoughts is Bryan Magee's *Popper* (Fontana, 1985). The most notable counterpoint to Popper's beliefs is found in Thomas Kuhn's 1962 book *The Structure of Scientific Revolutions* (University of Chicago, 1996), which views the history of science as being primarily driven by paradigm shifts. The debate is well worth exploring for yourself.

6 Creative and collaborative thinking

29 Ken Robinson, *Out of Our Minds: The Power of Being Creative* (Capstone, 2017), p. 2. If you want to find creative inspiration without leaving home, consider browsing some of the world's great museum collections online: the Vatican museums offer a virtual tour that includes the Sistine Chapel; others include the British Museum, Guggenheim New York, Prado and Louvre.

30 'Toni Morrison: Write, Erase, Do It Over', interview by Rebecca Sutton, *NEA Arts*, 2014, no. 4, p. 2, online at www.arts.gov/ stories/magazine/2014/4/art-failure-importance-risk-and-experimentation/toni-morrison; for an in-depth exploration of her writing life, see Morrison's *The Source of Self-Regard: Selected Essays, Speeches, and Meditations* (Knopf, 2019) or, for an introduction to her fiction, *Beloved* (Vintage, 1997).

31 For information on the general principles of Buchalter's research, and its particular application to UK primary schools' curriculum, see his 'Nurturing Creative Thinking' project at the Global Governance Institute www.globalgovernance.eu/work/projects/ nurturing-creative-thinking/.

32 Alexander Mackendrick, *On Film-making: An Introduction to the Craft of the Director* (Farrar, Straus and Giroux, 2004), p. xxiv. Mackendrick's ideas are discussed and brought to life in the educational series 'Mackendrick On Film' (edited by Paul Cronin) which can be viewed on TheStickingPlace channel on YouTube. Sequence 7, on the grammar of film, is a good place to start: www.youtube.com/watch?v=cWkKdQXE5Uo.

33 For a rich exploration of the nature of dialogue – and the difficulty of truly listening to others – David Bohm's 1996 book *On Dialogue* (Routledge, 2004) remains a classic. For a subtle, personal exploration of the complexities of communication and self-knowledge, psychotherapist Lori Gottlieb's *Maybe You Should Talk to Someone* (Scribe, 2019) is entertaining and compassionate in equal measure.

7 Thinking about numbers

34 Among the best introductions to statistics I've read is David Spiegelhaler's *The Art of Statistics: Learning from Data* (Pelican, 2019). Another accessible, smart and engaging introduction is Tim Harford's *How to Make the World Add Up: Ten Rules for Thinking Differently About Numbers* (Bridge Street Press, 2020). A host of interactive modules teaching probability and basic statistical concepts are available for free on the Khan Academy website at www.khanacademy.org and come highly recommended. Start with the Unit on Probability and take it from there.

35 Onora O'Neil's Reith lecture on 'Trust and Transparency' can be read in full online at www.bbc.co.uk/radio4/reith2002/lecture4.shtml and is reproduced in *A Question of Trust* (Cambridge University Press, 2002). For her and others' work on 'intelligent openness' see The Royal Society Science Policy Centre report 'Science as an open enterprise' (June 2012) at https://royalsociety.org/~/media/royal_society_content/policy/projects/sape/2012-06-20-saoe.pdf.

36 'Coronavirus (COVID-19) Infection Survey pilot: England, 31 July 2020. Initial data from the COVID-19 Infection Survey.' Online at www.ons.gov.uk/peoplepopulationandcommunity/healthandsocialcare/conditionsanddiseases/bulletins/coronaviruscovid19infectionsurveypilot/31july2020.

37 Williamson, E.J., Walker, A.J., Bhaskaran, K., et al. (2020) 'Factors associated with COVID-19-related death using OpenSAFELY', *Nature* 584, 430–436, https://doi.org/10.1038/s41586-020-2521-4.

38 For an example of how statistical analysis can be both profoundly revealing as a description of the world, and galvanizing as an account of what needs to be challenged and changed, Caroline Criado Perez's *Invisible Women: Exposing Data Bias in a World Designed for Men* (Vintage, 2020) exposes the degree to which much that is taken for granted as 'normal' is premised upon male rather than female bodies and experiences.

8 Technology and complexity

39 One of my favourite explorations of the fundamental differences between humans and machines – and the ways we can all-too-easily overlook these – remains Jaron Lanier's wise, concise and provocative *You Are Not a Gadget* (Penguin, 2011).

40 Timandra Harkness, 'How Ofqual failed the algorithm test', UnHerd, 18 August 2020, online at https://unherd.com/2020/08/how-ofqual-failed-the-algorithm-test.

41 Hannah Fry, *Hello World: How to be Human in the Age of the Machine* (Black Swan, 2019), p. 70. Fry's tweet about the exam algorithm was posted at 11:26AM on 17 August 2020 and is online at https://twitter.com/fryrsquared/status/1295306053916254210. A second important, accessible book exploring algorithmic bias and inscrutability is Cathy

O'Neil's *Weapons of Math Destruction: How Big Data Increases Inequality and Threatens Democracy* (Penguin, 2017).

42 Many of these biases are addressed in Safiya Umoja Noble's powerful book *Algorithms of Oppression: How Search Engines Reinforce Racism* (NYU Press, 2018). For a discussion of both algorithmic bias and practical strategies for its mitigation, Joy Buolamwini's November 2016 TEDxBeaconStreet talk 'How I'm fighting bias in algorithms' is well worth viewing at www.ted.com/talks/joy_buolamwini_how_i_m_fighting_bias_in_algorithms.

43 John Sterman, 'Making Systems Thinking More Than a Slogan', 5 November 2013, for the Network for Business Sustainability, online at www.nbs.net/articles/making-systems-thinking-more-than-a-slogan; when it comes to thinking systematically and holistically about complexity and the future, Kate Raworth's *Doughnut Economic: Seven Ways to Think Like a 21st-Century Economist* (Random House Business, 2018) is at the forefront of some urgent challenges to existing disciplinary boundaries.